When you know something extra!

PRIYAM GHOSH

About the Author

Mr. Ghosh is an experienced International Education consultant & career advisor. He helps students to choose a proper career option and course and he has in-depth knowledge of study options in top countries including UK, Australia, Canada, USA and so on. He has completed his Bachelor's from the University of Calcutta. He has also earned his Master's in Commerce.

Why I'm writing this book? & How this book will help you?

From my college days I started developing my interest in various subjects like Investment, Astrology, Spirituality, Stock Market and so on. To gain in-depth knowledge I started my research about various subjects and it helped me a lot at my initial stage. After that when I got my first job then I got the opportunity to invest in myself so that I can be a better version of myself. From that time, I started buying different books to enhance my knowledge. My initial target was to buy those bestselling or highly famous books so that I can learn something new. Truly speaking, those books are not just books, rather those are the Bible of leading a meaningful life.

It took me long time to complete a good number of international bestselling books. Now when I look back, I can realize that how much time I spent to learn about various things in detail but I don't regret about that, rather that time was one of the best times of my life.

Now the question is, does everyone have that much time to invest in themselves so that they can develop at least basic knowledge about a few subjects or topics which are very relevant to our life? Though we have time, but in majority of the cases we don't want to invest our time in reading books!

When it comes to gaining core knowledge about any specific subject then we need to study a lot and, in some cases, practical knowledge is must. But in this book, I've tried to give everyone fundamental knowledge about various subjects in a summarized way. Upon reading this book, you will get to know about various things. If you start researching about all those subjects which are covered in this book, it will take long time, only because of the variety of subjects and it will cost you a lot financially.

I have spoken to many people, who are keen to learn new things but at the same time they are busy with their profession, family responsibilities & academics. Finally, they are unable to allocate quality time to gain knowledge.

After considering everything, like time limitations, financial capacity, I'm writing this book. I can assure you, after reading each and every chapter or topic, you'll get a better and clear view about those topics.

Contents:

The Stock Market

When a thought regarding investment comes to our mind, then sometimes we consider investing in stock market. This is true that, it's one of the options of becoming rich within a short span of time. As it has the power to give extra-ordinary financial return.

Now, let's stop here and ask yourself one simple question:

How share market gives this much high return within a short time?

Most probably, as a new excited investor, you don't know the answer. But we should know the answer to protect our investment.

What is Stock Market actually & When investment in stock market is safe?

Stock market is a place, where we can give our money to a company and a company uses our money to maximise the company's value. Our money becomes their capital which they use for company's growth.

Now, as a new stock trader you may be earning 10% Return On Investment (ROI) in 2-3 days and most probably you have started considering yourself as an investor. But, are you an investor? The answer is No!

You are not an investor; you are a gambler and you're playing smart!

Becoming an investor in stock market is not that easy. It takes lot of time and patience, but you can also become an investor if you think logically.

When you are getting 10% return in 2-3 days, have you ever asked yourself that what is going wrong in the market? Because it's not possible for any big MNC to increase their company's value in 2-3 days, so, if you have invested some amount in a company then how can they give this much super-high return in just 2-3 days? Now the answer is simple. Actually, the company is not giving you this return in short-term, rather the stock market is giving you this return.

Because, the stock price is not always driven by logic or analysis, it's driven by emotion! and in any investment, where the return is driven by emotion is always a high-risk investment with super-high negative or positive return.

If the stock market is that much risky, then how so many people making their fortune on a consistent basis?

Yes, it's a valid argument!

Now just forget about stock market. Let me ask you a few questions...

If you get ill and you visit a doctor where doctor tells you that, he has two months of experience in this field. Though he doesn't have an MBBS but he has successfully diagnosed all the patients who visited him in last two months. Would you give him a chance?

Or, even a civil engineer without a B.Tech degree can get the chance to become your house building planner?

Never, right? Then how you can you think that without a proper degree / skill / knowledge, the stock market will give you a chance to become a king of the market? It's time to apply your common sense!

Can I make my fortune in stock market?

Answer is yes (without any doubt), you can. But the first step is to understand your need. Do you need high return in short time? Or are you thinking of long-term investment?

If you research about those stock market celebrities, then you will get to know that, most of these people believe in long-term investment and they will also suggest others to invest in top companies.

But, when you can get high return in short period of time from penny stock, then why this blue-chip stock?

Let's take an example:

You have INR.10K to invest in stock market. Now you can choose between penny stock of a small company/loss making company or you can go for blue-chip stock.

Case 1:

You brought the penny stock and earned 15% return in a week. As the share price was going up.

Case 2:

You invested in blue-chip stock and your return is only 2% in a week.

Now, if you have invested in penny stock then you may consider yourself as the winner. But are you really a winner? Let's understand this.

If you have already earned 15% return in a week time, then what will you do with that money? You can either wait for more return or you can sell your stock. If you wait, then chances are very high that you will suffer loss. If you sell your stock, then you will think of re-investing your amount. Now, if you continuously try new companies then also you will suffer loss, only because, the companies you're investing in, majority of the time they are loss making company and they don't have any business sustainability.

On the other hand, big companies usually don't give high return in short term. But in long term, the chances are high that you'll get good return. As these big companies are basically growing companies in term of new product addition or value addition. So, ultimately your investment will remain in a company who have reputation in the market.

Are you confused about the short-term profit still now? Can you still earn profit in short team?

The answer is again yes!

You can, but for that you need proper knowledge and skills. Once you have knowledge and skills, then you need some experience. But the mistake we make is, we watch some training videos and we consider ourself as knowledgeable trader. We need to change this attitude. Everything takes time.

Can I invest in stock market in a risk-free way?

Not possible! Because, big companies also make huge losses sometimes. Alternatively, if you don't have proper knowledge and experience, then you have another way open.

The way is Mutual Fund!

Mutual Fund is an option through which you can invest a small amount of money (that can be as low as INR. 500 or 1000 in let's say 50 top companies in India). That means, if you are selecting any top-rated mutual fund, then you should get high return (probability is high) as all of those companies are growing companies and they have profit sustainability. So, the risk will be considerably low as compared to direct investment in stock. Reason is simple, if your INR. 500 is getting invested in 50 companies and if 10 of them gives negative return, then also you will have 40 companies, who can earn you a positive return.

Interesting fact about stock market:

An incident of 1721 (more than 300 years back)

The greatest mathematician and one of the most influential scientists of all time, Sir Isaac Newton started inversing his money in stock market. Initially he made huge profit as he was the early investor of South Sea company. But in 1721, he faced a loss of GBP 20000. Can you imagine? One of the greatest mathematicians of the world couldn't save his money and after watching some stock analysis video, if we consider ourselves an expert, then what can happen to us?

How to choose career?

Taking a career decision is one of the toughest decisions that we all know. But to help you all, I have selected some case studies, which will help you take right career decision.

Case study 1:

Let's talk about a boy who earned his degree from IIT Kharagpur in Metallurgical Engineering.

Do you have any idea about Metallurgical Engineering?

Metallurgical Engineering is the study of metals. How metals can be safely transformed into products. Now, what should be job opportunities of a person who has Metallurgical Engineering degree?

We're discussing about Mr. Sundar Pichai, the COE of Google. Did he have any idea that he will be a world leader of a Technology company, when he was completing his B.Tech ?

Case study 2:

Let's discuss about another boy, who completed Electrical Engineering and became an engineer of Hewlett Packard and later on he became a world-famous monk. The person is one and only, Mr. Gour Gopal Das.

Case study 3:

The first woman to become the Chairperson of State Bank of India, Ms. Arundhati Bhattacharya joined SBI as a

Probationary Officer in 1977. After 36 years of service to SBI, she became the Chairperson of SBI.

Moral of the story, if you are not keen to pursue any highly-specific program, then you can choose any course or career options initially. Every profession is a good profession if you give importance to that profession. Gradually you will be able to find your interest that can have no link with your education. But then also you can do well. But if you have some specific goal, then you have to choose career carefully.

<u>Things to consider, before choosing a career option:</u>

When we start our career initially, then we thought of too many things regarding our career. We sometimes also think that we have chosen a wrong career and we will have to continue it rest of our life.

To a big extent, we're influenced by social media. Where we get to see too many motivational career quotes, which tells us "Always do what you love'' or "follow your passion" etc etc…

According to me, we should take circumstantial decision!

Let's take an example, you are a middle-class boy or girl and you just completed your graduation from an average college. Though you wanted to complete your master's as well, but your financial condition clipped your wings. Now, you joined a company as you need to help your family financially. When you need a job on an emergency basis, then can you become choosy about the job role or company? I think, No!

This is the story of a large number of middle-class boys/girls in our society. If you can relate to this, that means, you're on the same page. You have already chosen a career as you were searching for a job badly. But, does it mean, you will have to continue the same for your rest of life?

Obviously not!

I want to make you understand that choosing your initial career is not in your hand all the time. It basically happens based on our financial needs or social needs. But what you do in long run that matters the most!

If we gist a few points to consider before choosing a career, then I would give utmost preference to our financial needs. I heard many people to say that money doesn't matter all the time, when it comes to career and completely disagree with them. **Money does matter and it matters all the time.** If you are into some creative profession then you might think that your creativity matters the most. But in real life, you'll hardly get any importance in your professional life if you look like poor. Let me tell you, no one likes poor people, not even a poor person likes another poor person! This is the reality, if can understand it at your early career then you'll do great in your entire life. So, the point is, when you have the option to choose your career, then always choose something, which brings good amount of money in your pocket then you will start loving your career.

At the same time, if you are passionate about something, which may not give you good financial value, then you can also do that on your free time. But you should always maintain a steady cash flow from any profession, and it doesn't matter, whether you like that or not. Because you are parallelly doing something, which you love.

Now, if you have selected a profession just to fulfil financial needs then also it's not a big problem, because life is a long journey. If you have some specific goals and when you're very focused about the same then the world will give you that opportunity. But according to my research, every career is fine when it's giving you social respect, money in your pocket and a peaceful sleep at night.

The mistakes we make in our career:

From my experience and research, I'm going to list a few career mistakes, like:

We try to act like a professional at our early career

Professionalism doesn't mean that you have to act like a professional all the time. When you're at your early career stage then don't act like a professional before your seniors. You may look smart for some time but you will never get to learn the core business skills until and unless you surrender yourself.

Changing company too often

When we are at our initial career stage, we always think of short-term benefits. We keep changing companies for some comfort or financial benefits. But we miss the core knowledge. I can guaranty you; no boss will share his/her core knowledge with you when you don't have mental stability.

Doing multiple things along with a full-time job

Young generation always has a tendency to show up that they are a multi-tasker and they forget to allocate quality time to themselves.

Another big career mistake we make that we forget, gathering information is not knowledge. When we start our profession, we give too much time to that profession. Where we try to gather too much information and carry that in our head to impress others. But we have to remember that it's 2023 not 1923. The information we are gathering that is not sufficient for our career as this age is information age. Where an AI is thousand time smarter and accurate than us.

Apart from these, there are many other potential mistakes which we make in our careers, some examples include:

- We forget to build relationships with other people within our industry (As it gives benefits in future)
- Not continuing to learn and develop new skills which is actually needed in that industry
- Being too quick to quit a job or give up on a career path
- We try to copy others and we forget our goals
- Not being able to handle stress or pressure
- Not having a good work-life balance, as we try to show-off that we're a hard worker

According to me, if we can avoid all these things, then we can have a better career and great work-life balance. It's important to remember, that, <u>we should have time to spend our money otherwise life will become meaningless!</u>

Job vs. Business

I know this is one of the famous topics and almost everyone has some opinion on the same. But in this chapter, I'm not only going to discuss the advantages or disadvantages of job or business. Rather, let's understand what is a job and what is a business first.

Answer is too short according to my understanding;

Job needs your active involvement throughout your professional life but business is self-managed!

If business can make someone free, then why we run after job all the time?

Because you cannot do business, business happens. If you think that, there is something which doesn't need your patience, doesn't need your involvement and it will happen automatically, then only God can save you.

Business is all about skill development. If you can develop your skills then you can also start your business automatically, without having any office or capital.

Let's learn some business fundamentals with example:

Your age is 25 and you are a Data entry operator. You are doing data entry 9 hours a day and earning INR 400 on a daily basis. At the same time, you know that your company sells your work to another company where he gates INR. 550. That is INR. 150 is his profit as he has given you employment and job security.

Now your age is 28 and you have three years of data entry experience. You have gained good reputation in the market only because of your honest approach towards your job. One day you thought of starting your business and hired 4 people for the same data entry job. Now the case is different, as you are earning INR. 150 per person on a daily basis, so without doing anything you're earning INR. 600 per day.

Do you think, that it is a business? Of course not. Why? There is a reason:

Because you're now earning nominal amount and you're taking this much of high risk, which is meaningless.

You haven't developed your skills & started your business, then someone will outshine your business for sure.

When you're going to plan a business, never plan a business which is risk free, less expensive and easy to start. If you do so, then your smartest employee will become your biggest competitor in a short span of time.

Why some people always prefer to start their own business? & When you should start your own business?

I can say, deciding to start a business vs. working for someone else is a personal and complex decision that depends on a variety of factors. Here are some factors to consider when deciding if starting your own business is the right path for you:

Passion: If you have a particular passion or expertise, starting your own business can be a way to turn that passion into a career. Owning your own business can give you the freedom to pursue what you love and make a living doing it.

Flexibility: When you will start your own business, it will give you greater flexibility in terms of work schedule, location, and the types of work you take on. This can be especially appealing if you have personal obligations or interests that make it difficult to work a traditional work schedule.

Risk taking capability: Starting a business involves a significant amount of risk, including financial risk. You have to consider your own risk tolerance before deciding to start a business. You may be comfortable taking on more risk than others, or you may prefer the security of a steady pay check.

Skills and experience: Before starting your own business, always consider your own skills and experience and whether you have what it takes to run a successful business. Starting a business involves a wide range of responsibilities, from marketing and sales to accounting and operations & you have to do everything initially!

Market demand: Market demand is the most important thing for a business. Before doing anything, make sure there is a market for the product or service you want to offer. You can conduct market research to determine if there is a demand for what you want to provide and how you can differentiate yourself from your competitors.

Financial stability: Starting a business is generally expensive, and it may take good amount of time before you see a return on your investment. Make sure you have the financial stability to overcome any initial losses and support yourself and your family during the initial phase.

A **SWOT** analysis is a framework used to assess the Strengths, Weaknesses, Opportunities, and Threats of a business. It is a useful tool for a businessman, especially new ones, to analyse the internal and external environment and make informed decisions. Here's how you can conduct a SWOT analysis for your new business, along with some examples:

Strengths: This refers to the positive attributes of your business, such as its unique selling proposition (USP), competitive advantage, or talented team.

Examples of strengths for a new business could be:

- ✓ Proprietary technology or process that provides a competitive edge.
- ✓ Talented and experienced team members with industry knowledge.
- ✓ Unique product offering that solves a specific problem.

Weaknesses: This refers to the internal factors that could hinder the success of your business, such as a lack of resources, skills, or experience.

Examples of weaknesses for a new business could be:

- ✓ Limited financial resources for marketing and promotion.
- ✓ Lack of brand awareness and credibility in the market.
- ✓ Inadequate expertise or skills to handle complex operations.

Opportunities: This refers to external factors that can benefit your business, such as industry trends, emerging markets, or new technologies.

Examples of opportunities for a new business could be:

- ✓ Growing demand for your product or service due to market trends.
- ✓ Increasing consumer awareness and acceptance of your product or service.
- ✓ Emergence of new markets or technologies that can be leveraged for business growth.

Threats: This refers to some external factors that can negatively impact your business, such as economic downturns, competitors, or changes in regulations.

Examples of threats for a new business could be:

- ✓ Competitive landscape with large, established companies dominating the market.
- ✓ Changes in regulations or laws that can impact the business operations.
- ✓ Economic downturns or market uncertainties that can affect the business revenue.

<u>Here's an example of a SWOT analysis for a new fitness studio:</u>

Strengths:

- ✓ Unique fitness programs and services, targeting a niche market segment.
- ✓ Experienced and certified trainers and staff with industry knowledge.
- ✓ Prime location with easy accessibility and ample parking.

Weaknesses:

- ✓ Limited financial resources for marketing and promotional activities.
- ✓ Limited brand awareness and credibility in the market.
- ✓ Limited range of fitness equipment and facilities.

Opportunities:

- ✓ Growing demand for health and wellness services in the local market.
- ✓ Increasing popularity of fitness and wellness programs among the target audience.
- ✓ Partnerships with complementary businesses such as health food stores or wellness product suppliers.

Threats:

- ✓ Competition from existing established fitness studio in the area.
- ✓ Potential changes in regulations or tax laws that may impact the business operations / profit.
- ✓ Economic downturns or recessions that may result in reduced client's spending.

By conducting a SWOT analysis, you can identify your business strengths, weaknesses, opportunities, and threats, and make informed decisions about how to grow and improve their business.

Growth opportunities in business and job can be quite different, and the choice between the two depends on you:

Growth opportunities in Business:

When you own a business, you have the potential for unlimited growth opportunities. Your business can grow as big as you want it to, depending on your goals, strategy, and execution. You have control over the direction of the business and can make decisions that can drive growth and expansion. Owning a business can also provide opportunities to diversify and expand into new markets or new product lines.

Growth opportunities in Job:

In a job, growth opportunities typically come in the form of promotions, salary increases, and expanded responsibilities. You may also have the opportunity to learn new skills, work with new people, and take on different roles within the company. Depending on the company and industry, you may have the opportunity to work with new technologies, processes, and systems. Job growth opportunities are generally more stable and predictable than business growth opportunities.

Finally, we can say, if we want to have control over the direction of our growth, then owning a business may be the best option for us. If we prefer a more stable and predictable environment, and are satisfied with our current role and responsibilities, then pursuing growth opportunities within a job may be the best option for us. Ultimately, the choice between the two depends on our personal goals and priorities, as well as our risk tolerance and entrepreneurial spirit.

Now, coming to failure, both failure in a job and failure in a business can be dangerous, but the consequences and impact of failure can be different. Let's understand this....

Failure in a job:

When we fail at a job, we may lose our job, salary, benefits, and other perks that come with it. The failure may damage our reputation, making it harder to find a new job or grow our career.

However, the impact of failure is generally limited to our personal finances and career, and may not have a broader impact on the economy or society.

Failure in a business:

When we fail in a business, we may lose our entire investment, incur debts and liabilities, and damage our credit score (credit taking credibility). This failure may have broader economic and social impacts, such as job losses, disruption to supply chains, and loss of consumer confidence.

The impact of failure may also be felt by our employees, customers, suppliers, and other stakeholders, who may be affected by the closure of the business.

We can say, failure in a job can have a significant impact on our personal finances and career, but the impact is generally limited to our own life, nothing more than that. But failure in a business, on the other hand, can have broader economic and social impacts, and may affect the livelihoods of many people. Therefore, while failure in a job can be tough, failure in a business can be much more dangerous and should be approached with caution.

Spiritualty & Meditation

Spirituality can be termed as a sense of connection with the universe, henceforth it has its own importance. Spiritualty doesn't want us to become a monk but it gives us the clarity about our life and helps us to live a meaningful life. Spiritualty gives us the wisdom which makes us mature.

Spirituality refers to a person's sense of connection to something greater than themselves, and can often involve a search for meaning and purpose in life. It can include beliefs and practices related to a higher power, the divine, or the ultimate reality. Spirituality can be expressed through religious practices, such as prayer or worship, or through non-religious practices, such as meditation or mindfulness.

Spirituality can be a personal and subjective experience and can take many forms. Some people may find spirituality through traditional religious practices, such as praying, while others may find it through non-traditional practices such as meditation, yoga, nature walks, or mindfulness. Spirituality can also be experienced through art, music, dance and other forms of self-expression. That's why, it's important to have clear idea about Spirituality.

It can be a powerful source of comfort, strength, and guidance, helping people to find meaning and purpose in life, cope with difficult situations, and develop a sense of inner peace. It is a way to understand the meaning and purpose of life, and the relationship between oneself, others and the world.

<u>It is important to note that spirituality is not the same as religion, and that people may be spiritual without being religious.</u> Additionally, spirituality can be a personal and individual experience, and what is meaningful to one person may not be meaningful to another.

Coming to meditation, it's a process of achieving mental clarity. Which helps us to control our thoughts and emotions.

I believe majority of the educated people have the basic idea about spirituality and meditation. Therefore, we try to practise spirituality and often we try to meditate. We start thinking like a monk. Unfortunately, after a few days we find it difficult and we get back to our normal life, where we fight on small issues, we sought and it goes like that.

Have you ever thought, where we are making the mistake with spirituality?

Spirituality is nothing but the understanding of our life and it's all about understanding ourself and sadly the understanding of life is missing and we try to practise meditation or spirituality.

Let's understand it in a different way….

You are running your small business where you are dealing with customers on a daily basis. Naturally, you are facing big challenges with the customers, as they don't try to understand anything and they don't listen to you, they just argue. Now, after discussing your issue with some of your friends and well-wishers, you have started doing meditation on a daily basis, so that you can control your thoughts and emotions and you can have mental peace. Now what will happen? Do you think, it will solve all of your problems immediately?

If you want to solve your problem then you have to understand your problems. Our problem is, we try to solve those problems using meditation.

Let's take an example. You are an army officer and your duty is to protect our national border. In that case, if someone from other country attacks us, then it doesn't matter, how spiritual you are, you cannot practise your spirituality. If you do so, you will lose the fight. It clearly means that we, the common persons can only practise spirituality when everything going well.

Can meditation solve all of our problems?

Meditation can be a helpful tool for managing stress and improving overall well-being, but it is not a solution for all problems. While it has been shown to have many benefits, such as reducing anxiety and depression, improving focus and concentration, and increasing self-awareness. On the other hand, meditation alone may not be enough to address certain problems, such as financial difficulties or relationship issues. It is important to address these problems with a holistic approach, which may include seeking professional help, making changes to one's lifestyle and so on.

Meditation can be beneficial for a wide range of people and can be practiced by anyone regardless of their age, religion, or background. Some groups of people that may find meditation particularly beneficial include:

People who experience stress, anxiety, or depression: Meditation can help reduce symptoms of anxiety and depression and improve overall well-being.

People with chronic pain: Meditation has been found to help reduce pain and improve quality of life for people with chronic pain conditions.

People with insomnia or sleep problems: It can help improve sleep quality and increase feelings of relaxation.

Who wants to improve their focus: Meditation can help improve attention span and concentration.

Who want to develop self-awareness: Meditation can help increase self-awareness and improve emotional regulation.

People who want to improve their overall well-being: It can help improve overall well-being by reducing stress and promoting relaxation.

<u>Is there any real connection between spirituality and meditation?</u>

According to my research, there is a connection between spirituality and meditation, as both can involve a sense of connection to something greater than oneself, and can involve practices that promote inner peace, self-awareness, and a sense of purpose.

Meditation can be a spiritual practice for some people, as it can involve focusing on the present moment and connecting with one's inner self, which can lead to a deeper understanding of one's place in the world and a greater sense of meaning and purpose. Many spiritual traditions, such as Buddhism and Hinduism, include meditation as a central practice for achieving spiritual enlightenment. Meditation can also be a way for people to connect with their own personal sense of spirituality, regardless of whether or not they have a specific religious affiliation.

Saving Money & Investment

Money is something which gives us comfort & security. So, we are the common people, we try to save money. We save money according to our income. We save money in our savings accounts, we make FDs. But then also we fill in-secured about our financial conditions. I believe you can relate to this.

If this is true, then where we are making the mistake? Do we understand how money works?

If you have financial knowledge then you know about inflation. But is it the only reason of our financial insecurity? No!

Let's understand the basic financial crisis a person faces in his/her life…

When you are able to read this book, that means you're an educated person and most probably you're into some white-collar job or profession. Now, as a middle class or lower middle-class people, we have several financial illiteracies, that's why we often lose our hard-earned money and we feel insured in our every aspect of life.

Is that means, if we become financially knowledgeable, then we'll be financially free?

No, it's not that easy. I don't want to give you any false motivation. Who say they are finally free, in most of the cases, they are not financially free, they act like that, so that they can earn some extra money by motivating you. The reality is, becoming financially free is depends on different things, like your mindset, your work & your luck factor. You can't ignore any of these. Why? Let me explain:

Mindset: Our mindset is one of the most vital elements of becoming financially free. You work on something which can give you more than enough money and if your luck supports you, then also you need a right mindset towards your financial situation. Let's take an example, you are a well-qualified person, you're doing high paying jobs, and you're on INR. 24 Lacs CTC. Now after continuing your job for two years, you can see that you have already saved INR. 14 lacs only in two years. Now you started calculating that how much can you save in 10 years down the line. And the amount will be in crore. Here, you took a decision of buying a high-cost flat in a popular place which will cost you INR. 80 lacs, whereas you already have a flat, where you can live comfortably. But without giving it a second thought (just to match your living standard with rich people) you brought that on zero down payment as you know that, you have to pay a monthly instalment for next 15 years. Now your monthly EMI will be around INR 80K.

Now, you are living luxuriously, thinking that you are earning INR. 2 Lacs per month, whereas your actual salary is (2 Lacs – 80K) INR. 1.2 Lacs. Unfortunately, this is not the end of your loan.

When you are moving to a far better place & in a far better flat, then you not only change your address, you change your entire lifestyle too. Now, you are a part of rich society and you are meeting reach people on a daily basis.

Coming your previous lifestyle, you prefer pubic transport to go to office and your financial budget for your transportation was capped. Now, after a few days, you'll notice that the society you belong to, they don't use public transport, they have their own car. Now you need a branded car, a better TV etc etc. Within a few months, you will regret and will feel uncomfortable regarding your finance. Because, you are doing what the society wants you to do!

On the other hand, if you have a better mindset then you can also live a better life according to your income and savings.

Let's put yourself in the same condition, that you are earning INR. 2 Lacs per month. Now, just give it enough thought about your actual cashflow.

When you are earning INR. 2 Lacs per month, then that is not your actual income. Because you'll have a bigger tax liability. Let's take your in hand actual salary is INR.1.7 Lacs. Now before going to buy a new flat, you are doing your homework fast, so that you can take calculated risk.

Now, there are some ways, in which we lose our money. One of the biggest reasons is medical reason. Medical emergency is unpredictable. So, it doesn't matter, how much you are earning. A big medical emergency can make you bankrupt. To save yourself financially, you can take a proper medical insurance which may cost you and family 5K per month.

Apart from medical insurance, you have your family responsibility too and your family needs financial security. If you are doing job in any private company, then in majority of the cases, it's needless to say that you don't have any job security. So instead of having an unreal philosophy (that you are irreplaceable and your organization can't fire you) you can calculate your monthly household expenditure (including the EMIs you pay). If it's INR. 40K then if can save INR. 80K then it's your next two months expenditure, and it doesn't matter how many days of time your organization will give you when they are trying to replace you, but you can give yourself two more months to look for a better job. That means your family is partially secured (which is also rare in our economy). At the same time, you can also use that money for any emergency purpose, that can be any medical emergency in your family.

Now you have secured your family from any big medical emergency and you have money to support your family for next two months. But you have to buy a new flat, as you deserve that. At the same time, you also have to save some money for your future. That you can take for an example that it's INR. 20K per month (I know, the majority of the people even earn less than INR. 20K per month. But irrespective if your income, you can save some nominal amount).

Therefore, it is clear that you need to do lot of things apart from buying a new flat. So, when you have a right mindset and a clear understanding about life, then you will be in a better financial position. If we continue the same example, then when it comes to buying a new flat you can go for a better flat which suite your budget.

Your Work: It is needless to say that, your work has the most direct relationship with your cash flow. Henceforth, you should choose your career carefully. It doesn't matter which profession you are in; you can do something wonderful in any profession and can save a substantial amount to money in your life.

Now, if you choose any profession where you are easily replaceable or when you are running a business which is so easy that, anyone with a small budget can start, then your financial condition at a risk. If you do something meaningful in your career then you will get the value, otherwise not.

Luck factor: Our luck plays a vital role in our success; you can accept this fact or you can ignore it.

Savings and investments are both important financial tools, but they serve different purposes and have different characteristics. Let's understand the differences:

Savings: Savings refer to the money we set aside for future use. The primary goal of saving is to accumulate money for a specific purpose, such as emergency fund, a down payment on a house, or a vacation. Savings are typically held in a bank account or a savings account, which offers minimal interest rates. Some of the key characteristics of savings include:

- ✓ Low risk: Savings are considered low-risk investments because they offer low returns but with little risk of losing money. Our money is insured by the government up to a certain amount.
- ✓ Liquidity: Savings are highly liquid, meaning we can access the money quickly and without penalty. We can withdraw our money anytime without any restrictions.
- ✓ Low returns: Savings accounts typically offer low interest rates, so our money may not grow as fast as it would with other types of investments.
  Examples: Savings accounts, certificates of deposit etc.

Investment: Investments refer to the money we put into an asset or a venture with the goal of earning a higher return. The primary goal of investing is to grow our wealth over time, such as retirement savings or a long-term financial goal. Investments can be held in various forms, including stocks, bonds, mutual funds, real estate, and other types of assets. Some of the key characteristics of investments include:

- ✓ Higher risk: Investments carry higher risk than savings, as they can fluctuate in value and can result in losing money. Investments have a higher potential for returns, but also come with the risk of losses.
- ✓ Lower liquidity: Investments are less liquid than savings because they often have restrictions on when and how we can withdraw our money. Some investments may require a long-term commitment as well.
- ✓ Higher returns: Investments offer the potential for higher returns than savings, but with higher risk. Our money can grow much faster than in a savings account, depending on the type of investment we choose.

  Examples: Stocks, mutual funds, bonds etc.

If we compare Savings & Investment, then Savings are focused on short-term goals and are low risk with low returns, while investments are focused on long-term goals and can be higher risk but offer the potential for higher returns.

There are several reasons why common people may not fully understand the difference between savings and investment, like:

Lack of financial education: Financial literacy is not typically taught in schools, and many people do not have access to resources that can help them understand the basics of personal finance. As a result, people may not fully understand the concepts of savings and investment, or the different types of investment options available to them.

Confusing terminology: The financial industry can use complex and technical terms that may be difficult for the average person to understand. Terms like "mutual funds," "stocks," and "bonds" may not be familiar to many people, and they may not understand the differences between these investment options.

Lack of time and attention: People lead busy lives and may not have the time or energy to devote to learning about personal finance. As a result, they may rely on general knowledge or assumptions about savings and investment, without fully understanding the details or implications of these financial tools.

Coming to the conclusion, we need to consider Savings and Investment both the things together. If we only focus on savings then our money will lose its value because of inflation and if we invest all our money in high-risk zone, then we many face huge financial loss. Henceforth, we need to balance our savings and investment to create wealth.

Astrology

Astrology is one of the most controversial topics for common people as it's based on some belief system. Henceforth we always remain under dilemma that whether we should believe in it or not. But at the same time instead of doing own research we listen to our friends and relatives (who claims that he/she has got some benefits after wearing a gemstone) and we visit an astrologer and buy gemstones. After that, sometimes we get benefit and sometimes we get upset.

In this chapter, I will not give my conclusion that whether to believe in it or not, but I'll try to give you some insight about the fundamental concepts, which I got to know from some experts and I have done my personal research about Vedic astrology.

Vedic Astrology is mainly related to our past lives (Karma). Where we get our predictions based on the planetary positioning of stars when we were born. That means, when your planetary positioning is bad that means your previous life karma was not good and if the position is good that means, we did something meaningful in our previous lives.

Does it mean that it's unscientific?

If you take my opinion then I want to give it a logical approach. When a subject is being taught for thousands of years then it doesn't matter whether the subject has any scientific base or not. It is at least giving some benefits to us that we can be rest assured, otherwise this subject would have been abolished from the human history.

Why astrological predictions sometime match but sometime doesn't match?

Astrological predictions are based on the alignment of celestial bodies at the time of a person's birth and their perceived influences on that person's life. While astrology has been around for thousands of years and has a following of millions, it is not considered a science and is not supported by scientific evidence.

One reason why astrological predictions may not always match up with a person's life is that astrology is a very complex system that takes into account many different factors, such as the positions of the sun, moon, and planets at the time of a person's birth. It is also based on the interpretation of the astrologer, and not every astrologer may interpret the same chart the same way.

Astrological predictions are often general in nature and may not take into account a person's unique circumstances, personality, and life choices. People are complex and unique, and astrological predictions are not able to capture all the nuances of an individual's life.

Furthermore, the predictions are based on the assumption that celestial bodies, such as stars and planets, have an influence on human behaviour, which is not supported by scientific evidence. We have to remember that astrological predictions should be viewed as general guidelines rather than hard and fast rules, and that ultimately, people have free will and the power to shape their own lives.

History of Astrology:

Astrology is an ancient practice that dates back thousands of years, and its origins can be traced to the civilizations of Mesopotamia, Egypt, and India. The exact origins of astrology are not well-documented, but it is believed to have emerged from early human attempts to understand and interpret the movements of the stars and planets.

The Babylonians are considered to be the first civilization to develop a system of astrology, around the 2nd millennium BCE. They observed the movements of celestial bodies and recorded them in cuneiform tablets, which were used to predict future events and interpret the fate of individuals based on their birth date and the position of the planets.

Astrology then spread to other cultures and was adapted and refined over time. The ancient Egyptians also practiced a form of astrology, as did the Greeks and Romans, who borrowed heavily from the Babylonian system.

In India, astrology is a deeply ingrained part of Hindu culture and is known as Jyotish, which means "science of light." The Indian system of astrology is based on the sidereal zodiac, which is slightly different from the tropical zodiac used in Western astrology.

During the Middle Ages, astrology gained widespread popularity in Europe and was widely practiced by scholars, scientists, and rulers. Astrology was considered a legitimate field of study and was used to make predictions about political events, natural disasters, and personal fortunes. However, as scientific knowledge advanced and the enlightenment brought about a more rational and empirical approach to knowledge, astrology began to fall out of favour and was increasingly seen as a pseudoscience.

Despite this, astrology has persisted as a popular and widely practiced form of divination, and is still used by millions of people around the world to gain insight into their personalities, relationships, and future prospects. While astrology has been the subject of much scepticism and criticism, its enduring popularity suggests that it continues to fulfil a deep human need for meaning and guidance in a complex and unpredictable world.

It is not accurate to say that all smart Indians avoid astrology, as astrology continues to be a popular and widely practiced form of divination in India and other parts of the world.

One reason for this scepticism is the increasing availability of scientific and empirical methods for understanding the world. As people become more educated and exposed to scientific knowledge, they may be less likely to rely on traditional forms of divination, including astrology.

Another reason is the increasing awareness of the limitations and flaws of astrological predictions. While astrology can offer insights and guidance, it is not a precise or reliable method for predicting the future. Some people may choose to avoid astrology because they see it as a superstitious or irrational practice that has little basis in empirical evidence.

The rise of alternative forms of spirituality and self-improvement may have led some people to explore other methods for understanding themselves and their place in the world. Practices like mindfulness, meditation, and yoga have gained popularity in India and around the world, and may offer a more rational and evidence-based approach to personal growth and self-awareness.

Overall, the reasons why some Indians may choose to avoid astrology are complex and multifaceted, and reflect broader shifts in attitudes towards tradition, science, and spirituality in contemporary society.

Can a gemstone change our future?

There is no scientific evidence to support the idea that gemstones have the power to change a person's future. The belief that gemstones have certain properties that can affect a person's life is based on traditional and cultural practices, rather than scientific fact.

The practice of using gemstones for healing or to bring good luck is known as crystal healing and it's considered a form of alternative medicine. According to this belief, different gemstones have different properties, and each one is said to have a specific effect on the body, mind, and spirit.

Some people may believe that wearing certain gemstones can bring them good luck, health, or wealth. However, there is no scientific evidence to support this belief. Gemstones are just minerals, and they do not have any inherent power to change a person's future.

Gemstones can have a psychological effect on the person who wears them. They may feel good when they wear it, they may feel confident and positive, which can lead to change in their mood and behaviour.

Why common people waste lot of money on buying gemstone?

There are several reasons why some people may choose to spend money on buying gemstones. One reason is that gemstones have been used for centuries in traditional and cultural practices and are believed to have certain properties that can affect a person's life. People who believe in this may choose to spend money on buying gemstones in the hopes that they will bring them positive change in their life.

Another reason is that gemstones can be seen as a status symbol, and people may choose to buy them as a form of self-expression or to show off their wealth. Additionally, some people may see gemstones as an investment, believing that they will appreciate in value over time.

Some people may also find gemstones aesthetically pleasing and enjoy wearing them as jewellery. They may also have sentimental value to the person, it may be a gift from a loved one, it could be a ring from their ancestors, it could be a memory of a special event.

Lastly, people may be influenced by the marketing and advertising of gemstones, which can create a perceived value or importance of certain gemstones, and people may be willing to spend money on them without fully understanding the true value of the gemstone.

Water has Memory

The concept of water having memory is a controversial one, and there is much debate among scientists about whether it is possible. Some studies have suggested that water can retain information about substances it has come into contact with, while others have found no evidence to support this idea.

The idea of water memory is based on the work of French scientist Jacques Benveniste, who conducted a series of experiments in the 1980s and 1990s that appeared to show that water could retain a "memory" of substances it had been in contact with. One of Benveniste's most famous experiments involved diluting an antibody in water to the point where there were no longer any molecules of the antibody left in the solution. Benveniste then subjected the diluted solution to an electromagnetic field that was supposed to "imprint" the memory of the antibody onto the water molecules. When this "imprinted" water was then used to stimulate cells that would normally respond to the antibody, the cells showed the same response as if they had been exposed to the actual antibody. This result appeared to suggest that the water had retained a memory of the antibody even though there were no longer any physical molecules of the antibody present in the solution.

However, Benveniste's experiments were widely criticized for their lack of rigor and for the fact that they could not be replicated by other researchers. Many scientists pointed out that the effects that Benveniste observed could be explained by other factors, such as contamination or human bias. Nevertheless, the idea of water memory has continued to capture the imagination of some scientists and members of the public, and there have been other studies that have attempted to investigate this phenomenon.

One study that appeared to support the idea of water memory was conducted by a team of researchers led by **Nobel Prize-winning physicist Brian Josephson**. In this study, the researchers exposed water to a magnetic field and then froze it. When the water was thawed, it appeared to form crystals that were different from those formed by water that had not been exposed to the magnetic field. This result appeared to suggest that the water had retained a memory of the magnetic field.

Another study that appeared to support the idea of water memory was conducted by a team of researchers in Italy. In this study, the researchers exposed water to a solution of DNA and then removed the DNA from the solution. They then exposed the water to a polymerase chain reaction (PCR), which is a technique used to amplify DNA sequences. The researchers found that the water that had been exposed to the DNA solution amplified the DNA sequences more effectively than water that had not been exposed to the DNA solution. This result appeared to suggest that the water had retained a memory of the DNA even though the DNA had been removed from the solution.

However, both of these studies have been criticized for their lack of rigor and for the fact that they could not be replicated by other researchers. Many scientists remain sceptical of the idea of water memory, arguing that there is no plausible mechanism by which water could retain a memory of the substances it has come into contact with.

Finally, we can say while there is some evidence to suggest that water may have memory-like properties, the idea remains controversial and is not widely accepted within the scientific community. I believe, further research is needed to fully understand the properties of water and its potential ability to store and transmit information.

Lucky Objects

Do you have any LUCKY OBJECT?

Belief in lucky objects is a common phenomenon observed in many cultures around the world. Some people believe that certain objects or instruments bring good luck, success, or fortune to them. While there is no scientific evidence to support the idea that inanimate objects can possess supernatural powers, people may still attribute positive outcomes to their lucky instruments due to some psychological reasons.

One explanation for the belief in lucky objects is the concept of conditioning. People may associate their good fortune with an object or instrument they had at the time and form a positive emotional connection to it. Over time, the object becomes a symbol of their success or good luck. As a result, they may feel more confident or optimistic when they have the object with them, which in turn could improve their performance and increase their chances of success.

Another explanation is the placebo effect, which is the phenomenon where a person experiences a positive effect simply because they believe in the treatment or intervention they are receiving. In the case of lucky objects, people may believe that having the object with them will bring them good luck, and this belief alone can help boost their confidence and performance.

Furthermore, belief in lucky objects may also provide a sense of control and agency in uncertain situations. In situations where the outcome is not entirely within a person's control, the belief in a lucky object can provide a sense of comfort and stability, which may reduce anxiety and stress and enhance performance. That means, it's not a bad thing for us.

Finally, we can say that, the belief in lucky objects is not based on any scientific evidence, but it can have psychological benefits for individuals.

EMI Magic

The Equal Monthly Instalment (EMI) system for loan repayments was first introduced by The Singer Sewing Company, an American sewing machine manufacturer, in the late 1800s. The company began offering instalment plans to customers who wanted to purchase their sewing machines but could not afford to pay for them in one lump sum.

There are several reasons why people may choose to buy things on EMI:

Affordability: EMI plans allow people to purchase items that they may not be able to afford upfront.

Convenience: EMI plans allow people to pay for items over a longer period of time, rather than having to come up with the full amount at once.

Flexibility: EMI plans can be tailored to suit the buyer's budget and repayment schedule.

No collateral required: EMI plans are usually unsecured loans, so you don't have to put up any collateral to get the loan.

Easy availability: EMI plans are widely available, and easy to apply for.

Credit score: EMI plans can help people to improve their credit score, as long as the payments are made on time.

Urgent need: Sometimes people may have an urgent need for something, and EMI can be a quick way to get it without having to save up for it.

Buying things on EMI can also have its downsides, such as higher interest rates, and it's important to be aware of the terms and conditions of the EMI plan you're considering. It's always a good idea to carefully evaluate your financial situation and to make sure that you can afford the EMI payments before committing to a plan.

EMI (Equal Monthly Instalment) can affect your financial situation in a number of ways:

Increased debt: Taking on EMI loans can increase your overall debt, which can make it more difficult to manage your finances.

High-interest rates: EMI loans often come with higher interest rates than other types of loans, which can make them more expensive in the long run.

Limited cash flow: Paying EMI can limit the amount of cash you have available for other expenses, such as savings or investments.

Difficulty in repaying: If you're unable to make your EMI payments on time, it can lead to late fees and penalties, which can further strain your finances.

Credit score: Late or missed EMI payments can negatively impact your credit score, making it harder to get approved for other loans or credit in the future.

Limited flexibility: Once you've committed to an EMI plan, it can be difficult to adjust or cancel it, which can limit your flexibility to make changes to your finances.

We have to consider the long-term financial impact of taking on an EMI loan, and to make sure that you can afford the payments before committing to a plan.

Additionally, it's always a good idea to have a solid financial plan in place, including an emergency fund, to help you manage your finances and any potential challenges that may arise.

If I'm not wrong, then you have already got an idea about whether to buy things on EMI or not. Now let's talk about the ways to stay away from EMI.

Here are a few ways to avoid taking on EMI loans:

Save up for the purchase: Instead of taking on an EMI loan, try to save up the money to pay for the purchase in full. This can help you avoid interest charges and other fees associated with EMI loans.

Look for alternatives: Consider other options such as renting, leasing, or borrowing from friends or family.

Compare interest rates: If you do decide to take on an EMI loan, compare interest rates and terms from different lenders to find the best deal.

Prioritize your expenses: Make a list of your expenses and prioritize them according to their importance. Cut out unnecessary expenses and try to save money in order to avoid taking EMI loans.

Avoid impulse buying: Impulse buying can lead to overspending and taking on unnecessary EMI loans. Try to stick to a budget and only buy what you can afford to pay for in full.

Create an emergency fund: Building an emergency fund can help you manage unexpected expenses and avoid taking on EMI loans to cover them.

While EMI loans can make it easier to purchase big-ticket items, they can also come with high interest rates and fees, and can ultimately put a strain on your finances. By saving up and looking for alternatives, you can avoid taking on unnecessary debt and maintain control over your finances.

Education

It is possible for an illiterate person to become wealthy. There are several examples of successful entrepreneurs and business owners who did not have formal education but were able to build successful careers through hard work, determination.

However, having a basic education and strong literacy and numeracy skills can greatly benefit individuals in their personal and professional lives and increase their opportunities for success and financial stability. Let's understand, why education is so important...

A society with a large population of wealthy but uneducated individuals may face several problems, including:

- ✓ Lack of critical thinking and problem-solving skills, leading to poor decision-making
- ✓ Difficulty in adapting to a rapidly changing and complex world
- ✓ Limited contributions to society in terms of innovation and creativity
- ✓ Difficulty in promoting social and cultural understanding
- ✓ Lack of basic health and well-being knowledge, leading to increased health problems
- ✓ Limited understanding of the importance of education and its benefits, leading to reduced investment in education
- ✓ Increased likelihood of poverty and social inequality in future generations

- ✓ Difficulty in building a skilled and knowledgeable workforce to support economic growth and development.

Importance of education for children:

Education is crucial for children as it provides them with the foundation for their personal and professional development. Some of the key benefits of education for children include:

Cognitive Development: Education helps children develop their cognitive abilities, including critical thinking, problem-solving, and small decision-making skills.

Knowledge Acquisition: Children learn a broad range of subjects in school, including science, math, history, literature, and the arts, helping them build a strong foundation of knowledge.

Career Preparation: Education equips children with the skills and knowledge they need to pursue their chosen careers and achieve financial stability.

Social and Emotional Development: Education helps children develop social and emotional skills, including communication, teamwork, empathy, and self-esteem.

Civic Engagement: Education teaches children about their rights and responsibilities as citizens and helps them become active and informed members of society.

Health and Well-Being: Education provides children with the knowledge and skills they need to maintain their physical and mental health.

The existence of God

The existence of a deity is a philosophical and theological question that has been debated for centuries and remains a matter of personal belief. There is no scientific evidence proving the existence of a god, but many people find comfort and meaning in religious beliefs. Ultimately, the existence of a god is a question that may never be definitively answered.

The belief in a higher power or deity has existed in various forms since ancient times, across different cultures and civilizations. Evidence of religious beliefs and practices have been found from prehistoric times, including prehistoric rock art, burial practices, and offerings. The exact origin of belief in a god or gods is difficult to determine and likely arose as early human societies attempted to explain natural phenomena and the meaning of life.

People's belief or non-belief in a god or gods can be influenced by a number of factors, including:

Upbringing: Many people adopt the religious beliefs of their parents and community, which can shape their views on the existence of a deity.

Personal experiences: Some people may have had experiences that they interpret as evidence of a higher power, while others may have had experiences that lead them to doubt the existence of a god.

Reason and logic: Some people find arguments for the existence of a god compelling, while others find the same arguments unconvincing.

Culture: Culture and society can play a role in shaping religious beliefs, with some cultures and societies being more religious and others less so.

Ultimately, belief or non-belief in a god is a personal and subjective choice, influenced by a combination of individual experiences, emotions, and intellectual factors.

As mentioned earlier, there is currently no scientific evidence that proves the existence of a deity. Science, which relies on empirical data and observation, has not produced any conclusive evidence for the existence of a god. The existence of a god is considered a matter of faith and belief rather than a scientific fact.

Many religious people argue that the existence of a god can be inferred through the complexity and order of the universe, or through personal experiences and intuition. However, these arguments are not considered scientifically verifiable.

Now, whether or not to believe in a god is a personal decision that each individual must make for themselves. There is no right or wrong answer, and people have different reasons for why they choose to believe or not to believe.

Social influence

Social influence is the impact that people have on one another's thoughts, feelings, and behaviors. It refers to the ways in which people's opinions, beliefs, and actions are affected by the presence or actions of others.

<u>Social influence can have positive effects. It can lead to:</u>

Improved decision-making: By considering the opinions and perspectives of others, individuals can make more informed decisions.

Increased social cohesion: By conform to social norms, individuals can feel a greater sense of belonging to a group, and improve their relationships with others.

Greater creativity and diversity: Social influence can encourage individuals to try new things and think outside the box.

Better group performance: By combining the strengths and abilities of group members, social influence can lead to better results than those achieved by individuals working alone.

Increased compliance with important rules and laws: Obedience to authority can help ensure compliance with important laws and regulations, promoting social order and stability.

At the same time, it's important to note that social influence can also have negative consequences, such as limiting individuality and promoting conformity, leading to misinformation and harmful behaviour, and reinforcing existing power dynamics.

Negative social influence:

There are several examples of negative social influence, including:

Groupthink: The tendency of group members to conform to the opinions of the group, even if they are not in line with their own beliefs. This can lead to poor decision-making and a lack of creativity. For example, a group of executives may ignore dissenting opinions and make a poor business decision based on the prevailing attitude of the group.

Mob mentality: The phenomenon where individuals in a group behave in ways that they would not normally behave as individuals. This can lead to aggressive and harmful behaviour. For example, a crowd at a sporting event may start a riot because of the influence of the group dynamic.

Conformity to harmful norms: Individuals may conform to harmful norms, such as discriminatory attitudes and behaviours, due to the influence of the group. For example, peer pressure can lead individuals to engage in dangerous or illegal activities, like drug use.

Overestimating popular opinion: Social proof can lead individuals to overestimate the popularity of certain attitudes or behaviours. For example, individuals may assume that everyone supports a particular political candidate because of the media attention they receive.

Pressure to conform to beauty standards: Social comparison can lead individuals to feel pressure to conform to unrealistic beauty standards set by media and popular culture. This can lead to negative body image, low self-esteem, and disordered eating behaviours.

Should you control the social influence on you?

It depends on the context and the specific type of social influence. In some cases, social influence can be beneficial and can help you make better decisions or improve your relationships with others. In other cases, it can be harmful and lead to negative consequences.

In general, you have to be aware of the influence of others and to critically evaluate the information and opinions that you receive from others. This can help you make informed decisions and avoid being influenced by harmful or incorrect information.

However, you can not completely isolate yourself from social influence, as social interaction and exchange of ideas can be valuable for personal growth and development. Striving for a balance between being influenced by others and maintaining your own individuality can be a helpful approach.

<u>Here are some strategies that can help reduce the negative effects of social influence:</u>

Develop a strong sense of self: Having a clear understanding of your values, beliefs, and goals can help you resist negative social influence and make decisions that align with your own interests.

Surround yourself with positive influences: Seek out relationships with people who support and encourage you, and who have positive attitudes and behaviours.

Practice critical thinking: Evaluate the information and opinions that you receive from others, and seek out evidence to support or refute claims.

Seek out alternative perspectives: Encourage diversity of thought by seeking out different perspectives and opinions. This can help broaden your understanding and reduce the impact of groupthink.

Learn to say no: It's important to set boundaries and assert yourself when faced with negative social influence. Saying no to peer pressure or harmful social norms can be difficult, but it's important to stand up for what you believe in.

Focus on your goals: Keeping your goals and aspirations in mind can help you resist negative social influence and stay true to yourself.

Seek support: If you're struggling with negative social influence, seeking support from friends, family, or a mental health professional can be helpful.

Unhealthy self-esteem vs Healthy self-esteem

Unhealthy self-esteem is characterized by negative and unrealistic beliefs about oneself, and can lead to feelings of inadequacy, insecurity, and low self-worth. This type of self-esteem is often based on external validation, such as seeking approval from others, and is easily shaken by criticism or failure. Examples of unhealthy self-esteem include constantly comparing oneself to others, engaging in negative self-talk, and placing an excessive emphasis on achievement and success.

On the other hand, healthy self-esteem is characterized by a positive and realistic self-image, and a sense of self-worth and confidence. This type of self-esteem is based on internal validation, such as self-acceptance and self-appreciation, and is less affected by criticism or failure. Examples of healthy self-esteem include recognizing and accepting personal strengths and weaknesses, engaging in positive self-talk, and striving for personal growth and self-improvement.

It's our duty to strive for healthy self-esteem, as it can contribute to overall well-being and positive mental health outcomes, such as increased resilience, better relationships, and greater life satisfaction. Additionally, healthy self-esteem can also help to mitigate the negative effects of stress and adversity, and provide a foundation for personal growth and fulfilment.

<u>Here are some steps to help you determine whether you have positive or negative self-esteem:</u>

Evaluate your self-talk: Pay attention to the language you use when thinking about yourself, and notice if you tend to engage in negative self-talk, such as criticizing yourself harshly or focusing on personal flaws.

Assess your reaction to criticism: Consider how you typically react to criticism or failure. Do you have a tendency to internalize negative feedback and feel inadequate, or are you able to accept it objectively and use it as a learning opportunity?

Reflect on your personal values: Think about the values and beliefs that are important to you, and consider whether you feel that you live in accordance with them. Do you feel proud of who you are, or do you struggle with feelings of shame or guilt?

Analyse your relationships: Consider the relationships you have with others, and think about how you feel about yourself in these relationships. Do you feel worthy of love and respect, or do you often feel inadequate or inferior?

Seek feedback: Ask friends, family for their perceptions of you, and consider their feedback objectively. Be open to hearing both positive and negative feedback, and use it to gain a more accurate understanding of your self-esteem.

By evaluating your thoughts, behaviours, and relationships, you can gain a better understanding of your self-esteem, and identify any areas where you may need to work on building a more positive self-image. Additionally, seeking the help of a mental health professional, such as a counsellor or therapist, can provide additional support and guidance in this process.

It is also possible to convert negative self-esteem into positive self-esteem. Here are some steps that can help:

Challenge negative thoughts: Replace negative self-talk with positive affirmations, and question the validity of negative thoughts and beliefs.

Practice self-compassion: Be kind and understanding towards yourself, and recognize that everyone experiences failure, criticism, and disappointment.

Focus on personal strengths: Identify your personal strengths, and spend time celebrating and focusing on them.

Engage in activities that promote self-confidence: Engage in activities that you enjoy, and that make you feel confident and capable.

Surround yourself with positive relationships: Seek out supportive and positive relationships, and limit time spent with people who contribute to feelings of low self-esteem.

It takes time and effort to build positive self-esteem, and it's a journey that requires patience and persistence. However, by focusing on self-compassion, self-reflection, and personal growth, it is possible to develop a more positive self-image and increased feelings of self-worth and confidence.

Buying lottery tickets

Lottery tickets have been a source of hope and excitement for many people for decades. The idea of winning a large sum of money and being able to change one's life for the better has drawn millions of people to buy lottery tickets. But is buying a lottery ticket a wise investment to change our future?

Winning a lottery can provide an escape from the daily grind of life and offer a glimpse of hope for a better future. For people struggling financially, the dream of winning the lottery can provide a sense of comfort and optimism. It is a form of entertainment, and the anticipation of waiting for the numbers to be drawn can be a thrilling experience.

However, we should recognize that buying a lottery ticket is not a guarantee of financial success. The odds of winning the lottery are often very low, and for the majority of people who buy tickets, the investment does not pay off. In fact, for many people, buying lottery tickets can become a harmful habit, leading to overspending and financial difficulties.

In addition to the financial risks, buying lottery tickets can also contribute to a distorted perspective on wealth and success. It can perpetuate the idea that financial success is only attainable through chance and luck, rather than hard work and determination. This can lead to a negative impact on personal motivation and drive, as people may become too focused on the possibility of winning the lottery, rather than taking control of their financial future.

In conclusion, while buying a lottery ticket can provide a sense of excitement and hope, it is not a reliable or responsible way to change one's future. Instead of relying on luck, people should focus on developing healthy financial habits, such as budgeting, saving, and investing, which are more likely to bring long-term financial stability and success. In the end, taking control of our financial future requires hard work and dedication, not the purchase of a lottery ticket.

<u>Breaking a habit of buying lottery tickets can be challenging, but it is possible with a structured plan and determination.</u> Here are some tips that can help:

Identify the triggers: Take some time to reflect on why you buy lottery tickets. Is it boredom, stress, or a desire for quick financial gain? Understanding the reasons behind the behaviour can help you to find alternative coping mechanisms.

Set realistic goals: Focus on what you want to achieve in the long term, and make a plan to reach those goals. This will give you a sense of purpose and direction, and will help you to avoid the temptation to buy lottery tickets.

Find alternative activities: Instead of buying lottery tickets, find alternative activities that can bring you joy and excitement, such as taking up a new hobby or going on a trip.

Seek support: Surround yourself with friends and family members who support your goal to stop buying lottery tickets. They can offer encouragement and accountability.

Avoid temptation: Limit your exposure to lottery advertisements, and try not to visit places where lottery tickets are sold.

Practice self-care: Taking care of your physical and mental health is important for breaking any habit. Make time for exercise, healthy eating, and activities that bring you peace and happiness.

Breaking the habit of buying lottery tickets requires effort and determination, but with the right approach, it can be done. By focusing on alternative goals and activities, and seeking support from others, you can overcome the urge to buy tickets and work towards a brighter financial future.

Overthinking

Thinking and overthinking are two distinct processes of the mind, but they can be easily confused. Thinking is a normal and natural process of the mind that helps individuals make sense of their experiences, solve problems, and make decisions. Thinking is a useful tool for navigating life and is essential for personal growth and development.

On the other hand, overthinking is a pattern of excessive and repetitive thinking that can interfere with daily functioning and well-being. Overthinking is characterized by persistent and excessive rumination about events, experiences, or decisions, often leading to negative thoughts and feelings. This excessive thinking can be unproductive, leading to indecision, stress, and anxiety.

For example, thinking about a situation at work that requires a decision, such as whether to accept a job offer or decline it, is normal and healthy. On the other hand, overthinking about the situation, such as obsessing over the potential consequences of the decision and considering every possible outcome, can lead to stress and anxiety and prevent an individual from making a decision.

Another example of overthinking is ruminating over past events, such as a failed relationship. Normal thinking about past experiences would involve reflecting on what went well and what could be improved upon in the future, whereas overthinking might involve constantly revisiting the relationship, ruminating over what went wrong, and obsessing over the emotional pain caused by the breakup.

In conclusion, while both thinking and overthinking are normal processes of the mind, overthinking can lead to negative consequences and interfere with daily functioning. By recognizing the difference between the two and learning to manage overthinking, individuals can cultivate a healthier and more productive mindset.

Controlling overthinking is important for several reasons:

Mental Health: Overthinking can lead to increased stress and anxiety, which can negatively impact a person's mental health.

Decision Making: Overthinking can interfere with decision making by causing indecision, doubt, and confusion.

Productivity: Overthinking can prevent individuals from taking action and moving forward with their goals, leading to decreased productivity and satisfaction.

Relationships: Overthinking can also affect personal relationships by causing feelings of guilt, shame, and low self-esteem.

Quality of life: Overthinking can impact a person's overall quality of life by causing feelings of sadness, hopelessness, and helplessness.

Finally, controlling overthinking is important for maintaining good mental health, making effective decisions, increasing productivity, and improving relationships and overall quality of life.

Here are some tips and techniques to help stop overthinking:

Practice mindfulness: Focus on the present moment and engage in activities that bring you joy and relaxation.

Example: Try meditation or deep breathing exercises to calm your mind and bring awareness to the present moment.

Challenge your thoughts: Identify and challenge irrational or unhelpful thoughts that contribute to overthinking.

Example: When you catch yourself overthinking, ask yourself if the thoughts are based on facts or if they are just worry-based scenarios.

Engage in physical activity: Exercise can help to relieve stress and reduce negative thinking patterns.

Example: Go for a walk, do yoga, or take a fitness class to help distract yourself from overthinking.

Get enough sleep: Sleep plays a crucial role in mental health and can help reduce stress and anxiety.

Example: Establish a bedtime routine and stick to it to ensure you are getting adequate sleep each night.

Limit stimulation: Reduce exposure to negative or stressful stimuli, such as news or social media.

Example: Set aside time each day to disconnect from screens and engage in quiet activities, such as reading or listening to music.

It takes time and practice to stop overthinking, so be patient and kind to yourself as you work on developing new habits and thought patterns.

Spending time with people who don't give you importance

Spending time with people who don't give us importance can have a negative impact on our self-esteem and well-being. This behaviour can stem from a variety of psychological factors, including a need for validation and social acceptance, low self-esteem, and a fear of being alone.

For some people, the need for validation and social acceptance is so strong that they will tolerate being treated poorly in order to feel like they belong to a group or have friends. Low self-esteem can also play a role, as individuals may feel that they are not deserving of better treatment and are willing to accept mistreatment from others. The fear of being alone can also drive individuals to spend time with people who don't give them importance, as they may feel that it's better than being alone.

However, spending time with people who don't give us importance can have long-term negative effects on our self-esteem and well-being. It can lead to feelings of worthlessness and insecurity, and can contribute to the development of depression and anxiety.

In order to overcome this issue, it is important to recognize the value of our own worth and to seek out relationships that are based on mutual respect and support. This may involve setting boundaries with individuals who treat us poorly and making the difficult decision to end toxic relationships. Additionally, working on building self-esteem and seeking therapy can be helpful in overcoming the psychological factors that drive this behaviour.

To understand who gives you true importance and who is just acting, there are a few things to consider:

Quality of interaction: People who truly value you will make time for you, listen to you, and show genuine interest in your life. On the other hand, people who act like they value you may be less attentive and engaged in your conversations.

Consistency: People who truly value you will be consistently there for you, even when times are tough. Those who only act like they value you may be more sporadic in their attention and support.

Actions: People who truly value you will often go out of their way to show it through their actions. They may offer help or support without being asked, or make an effort to be there for you in difficult times.

Respect: People who truly value you will show respect for your feelings, opinions, and choices. Those who only act like they value you may dismiss or ignore your thoughts and feelings.

By paying attention to these factors, you can start to get a clearer understanding of who truly values you and who is just acting. It's also important to remember that not everyone will value you in the same way or to the same degree, and that's okay. The most important thing is to surround yourself with people who treat you with respect and kindness, and to let go of those who don't.

It can be difficult and lonely when you feel like no one gives you importance. However, there are steps you can take to improve your situation:

Focus on self-care: When you're feeling low, it's important to take care of yourself. Engage in activities that bring you joy, like reading, exercising, or spending time in nature.

Cultivate supportive relationships: Surround yourself with people who do value you, whether it's friends, family members, or support groups. Building a network of people who care about you can help to counteract feelings of isolation and neglect.

Improve your self-esteem: When you feel good about yourself, it's easier to let go of the opinions of others. Work on building a strong sense of self-worth and confidence through self-reflection and self-care.

Pursue your passions: Focus on your goals and interests. Pursuing what you're passionate about can give you a sense of purpose and fulfilment, even if others don't seem to value you.

Our self-worth is not dependent on the opinions of others. You are valuable and deserving of respect and love, no matter what others may say or do.

Your appearance does matter

The power of our appearance is demonstrated in the impact it can have on how people perceive and interact with us. For example:

Job Interviews: A well-groomed and professional appearance can create a positive impression during a job interview, which can lead to a job offer.

Social Interactions: People often form first impressions based on appearance, which can influence the level of trust, respect, and attention they give us.

Business Meetings: In a business setting, appearance can communicate professionalism and influence the level of confidence people have in our abilities.

Personal Relationships: A well-maintained appearance can attract people and create a positive image, which can be beneficial in romantic and social relationships.

In each of these examples, the power of appearance lies in its ability to impact how people perceive and interact with us, which can have a significant impact on our personal and professional lives.

<u>Maintaining a good appearance can have several benefits, including:</u>

Improved self-confidence and self-esteem: When you look good, you feel good, which can boost your confidence and self-esteem.

Positive first impressions: People tend to form initial impressions based on appearance, so maintaining a good appearance can help you make a positive first impression in personal and professional settings.

Professional advantages: In many professions, a well-groomed appearance is expected and can lead to advancement opportunities.

Increased likability: Studies have shown that people are more likely to be liked and treated positively by others if they maintain a neat and professional appearance.

Improved health: Taking care of your appearance can also improve your overall health, such as maintaining a healthy weight, good hygiene, and grooming practices.

While appearance is important, it's also crucial to recognize that it's not the only factor that defines a person's worth and that everyone has their own unique beauty and qualities.

Having a bad appearance does not guarantee a lack of importance in society. However, it can impact how people perceive and treat you, which can negatively affect your social and professional relationships.

We should remember that appearance is just one aspect of a person and does not define their worth or value as a human being. Personal qualities such as kindness, intelligence, and competence are often more important in determining a person's importance and impact in society. Additionally, it's important to focus on inner growth, self-improvement, and developing strong relationships and connections with others, as these are key factors in contributing to one's importance in society.

Here are some tips to help you maintain a good appearance:

Practice good hygiene: This includes regular showers, brushing your teeth, and keeping your hair clean and styled.

Dress appropriately: Choose clothing that is appropriate for the occasion, fits well, and is clean and wrinkle-free.

Keep your skin healthy: Use a gentle cleanser, moisturize daily, and protect your skin from the sun.

Exercise regularly: Regular exercise can help you maintain a healthy weight and improve your overall physical appearance.

Get enough sleep: Adequate sleep can help reduce dark circles and puffiness under the eyes, and improve the appearance of your skin.

Stay hydrated: Drinking plenty of water can improve the appearance of your skin, making it look more radiant and refreshed.

Keep your hair trimmed and styled: Regular haircuts and styling can keep your hair looking healthy and maintain its natural shape.

Take care of your nails: Keeping your nails trimmed, clean, and polished can help maintain a polished overall appearance.

Accessorize wisely: Adding the right accessories, such as jewellery, belts, can enhance your overall appearance and make you look put-together.

Spending too much time with gadgets

According to recent studies, technology addiction, specifically smartphone addiction, has become a widespread problem. Some statistics on this include:

In 2019, a survey found that 66% of people check their phone at least once every hour.

A study in 2020 found that 60% of smartphone users said they couldn't go a single day without their device.

Another study found that approximately 15% of people exhibit signs of technology addiction.

A 2020 survey of teenagers found that 89% of them felt they spent too much time on their devices.

These statistics highlight the growing issue of gadget addiction and the need for people to find a balance in their technology use.

Spending excessive amounts of time with gadgets can have both positive and negative effects. On the one hand, technology can provide access to information, entertainment, and social connections that can improve our quality of life. However, excessive gadget use can also have negative impacts on our physical, mental, and social well-being. Some of the negative effects include:

- ✓ Physical health problems such as eye strain, headaches, and neck/back pain
- ✓ Impairment of social skills and relationships due to decreased face-to-face communication

- ✓ Mental health issues like anxiety, depression, and sleep disorders
- ✓ Decreased productivity and focus due to distractions
- ✓ Addiction and dependence on technology

Therefore, it is important to use gadgets in moderation and find a balance between technology use and other activities such as exercise, socializing, and rest.

An example of how people can become addicted to gadgets is through the use of social media and smartphone technology. Social media platforms use various techniques such as notifications, likes, and endless scrolling to keep users engaged and coming back for more. Over time, this constant engagement can train the brain to crave the stimulation provided by these devices and create a cycle of dependence.

For example, a person may check their phone several times a day for new notifications and updates. Over time, this behaviour becomes automatic and the person may feel anxious or uneasy when they are unable to check their phone. Eventually, this constant phone checking becomes a habit that is difficult to break and the person may find themselves spending more and more time on their device, even when it's not necessary.

We have to be aware of this type of addiction and take steps to manage it. This can include setting limits on technology use, avoiding phone use before bedtime, and finding alternative activities to occupy your time.

Gadgets, especially smartphones and social media, use various psychological techniques to keep users engaged and coming back for more. Some of these include:

Variable reinforcement: Social media platforms like Facebook, Instagram, and Twitter provide unpredictable rewards in the form of likes, comments, and notifications, which can train the brain to keep checking for more stimulation.

Fear of missing out (FOMO): The constant updates and notifications from social media can create a sense of urgency and the fear of missing out on important events or information.

Endless scrolling: Social media platforms are designed to keep users scrolling and engaging with content for as long as possible. This can create the illusion of infinite content and make it difficult for users to break away from their device.

Bright colours and attention-grabbing graphics: Gadgets use bright colours, flashing lights, and attention-grabbing graphics to draw the user's eye and keep them engaged.

These techniques play on our psychological desires for rewards, social connection, and information and can make it difficult to put down our devices and break away from technology. It's important to be aware of these tactics and make conscious decisions about our technology use to avoid becoming addicted.

Gadgets, especially smartphones, can have a negative impact on our social lives in several ways. Here is an example:

People are spending more time on their devices, checking social media and texting with friends, instead of engaging in face-to-face conversations. This can lead to a decline in communication skills, emotional intelligence, and overall social skills.

For example, imagine a group of friends who used to spend time talking and hanging out in person. Now, they are more likely to spend time on their devices, scrolling through social media, and sending text messages to each other, instead of having face-to-face conversations. Over time, this can lead to a decline in their social skills, emotional intelligence, and the quality of their relationships.

It is important to be mindful of our gadget use and find a balance between technology and in-person social interactions. Setting limits on technology use, such as turning off notifications, can help reduce its impact on our social lives. Making time for face-to-face socializing, such as having dinner with friends or going for a walk, can help maintain and strengthen our relationships.

Artificial Intelligence & you

Artificial Intelligence (AI) refers to the development of computer systems that can perform tasks that would typically require human intelligence, such as recognizing speech, making decisions, and understanding natural language. AI technology has the potential to greatly benefit human society, but it also raises important ethical and social questions.

Here is an example of how AI relates to human beings:

Healthcare: AI can be used to analyse large amounts of medical data to help doctors diagnose and treat diseases more effectively. For example, AI algorithms can be used to analyse MRI images to detect signs of cancer, or to predict which patients are at high risk of developing certain conditions.

Employment: AI has the potential to automate many jobs, leading to job loss for some workers, but it can also create new jobs in areas such as data analysis and AI development. For example, a customer service representative might be replaced by an AI chatbot, but new jobs may be created for people who train and maintain the chatbot.

Personalization: AI can be used to personalize services and experiences for individual users, such as suggesting products or services based on their preferences. For example, a music streaming service might use AI algorithms to recommend new songs based on a user's listening history.

AI has the potential to transform many aspects of society, and it is important to consider both the benefits and risks as we continue to develop and integrate these technologies into our lives.

Artificial Intelligence (AI) has come a long way in recent years, but there are certain qualities that are unique to human beings that AI systems will never possess:

Empathy: AI systems lack the capacity to understand or share the feelings of others, which is a crucial aspect of human interaction and emotional intelligence.

Creativity: AI systems are not capable of generating new and original ideas or concepts in the same way that humans can.

Free will: AI systems are programmed to follow specific rules and algorithms, but they lack the capacity for independent thought and decision-making.

Moral judgement: AI systems do not have the ability to make moral or ethical decisions in the same way that humans do. They can be programmed to follow ethical guidelines, but they do not have the capacity to understand the reasoning behind these guidelines.

Emotional intelligence: AI systems lack the capacity for emotional intelligence and understanding, making them unsuitable for certain types of jobs such as counselling or therapy.

Sense of humour: AI systems cannot understand humour or sarcasm in the same way that humans do.

These qualities are integral to what it means to be human, and it is unlikely that AI systems will ever be able to replicate them fully. It is important to keep this in mind as we continue to develop and integrate AI into our lives and society.

Your uniqueness is your identity

Every human being is unique in their own way. No two individuals have exactly the same combination of personality, experiences, and perspectives. Our differences, whether they be physical, intellectual, emotional, or cultural, make us who we are and contribute to our individuality and uniqueness. While there are certainly similarities and common traits among people, each person is a unique combination of qualities and characteristics that makes them distinct from everyone else.

Discovering your uniqueness can be a journey of self-discovery and exploration. Here are some steps that may help:

Reflect on your experiences and memories: Think about the experiences and events in your life that have shaped who you are. Consider what makes you unique, what sets you apart from others, and what you are proud of.

Explore your interests and passions: Discover what you enjoy doing and what drives you. Consider what you are good at, what brings you joy, and what makes you feel fulfilled.

Get to know yourself: Take the time to understand your thoughts, emotions, and beliefs. Reflect on what is important to you, what your values are, and what you stand for.

Seek feedback from others: Ask friends, family, and colleagues for their thoughts and opinions on what makes you unique. Consider what they say and how it aligns with your own self-perception.

Try new things: Take on new challenges and experiences to broaden your horizons and discover new aspects of yourself.

Practice self-compassion: Be kind and understanding with yourself as you explore your uniqueness. Recognize that everyone has strengths and weaknesses and that there is no right or wrong way to be unique.

Discovering your uniqueness is a lifelong journey, and it can take time and effort to understand and fully embrace who you are. Be patient and compassionate with yourself, and enjoy the process of self-discovery.

Copying others takes away from your own individuality and creativity, and it can lead to feelings of insecurity and lack of self-worth. Instead of copying others, focus on discovering your own strengths, passions, and interests, and use those to create your own path in life.

Embracing your own uniqueness and individuality can bring a sense of fulfilment and purpose, and it allows you to create meaningful and authentic relationships with others. So, it is better to strive to be your true self, rather than trying to copy others.

Inferiority & superiority complex

Inferiority complex refers to a feeling of inadequacy and self-doubt that results in an individual feeling inferior to others. This can lead to a person feeling insecure and lacking confidence in their abilities and worth. Examples of this complex can be seen in individuals who constantly compare themselves to others and feel inadequate, those who avoid taking risks or trying new things out of fear of failure, and those who constantly seek validation from others.

Superiority complex, on the other hand, refers to a belief in one's superiority over others. This can manifest as arrogance, haughtiness, and a sense of entitlement. People with a superiority complex often believe they are better than others and may look down on those they perceive as inferior. Examples of this complex can be seen in individuals who believe they are smarter or more talented than others, those who constantly talk about their accomplishments, and those who dominate conversations and relationships.

It's important to note that both complexes can negatively impact a person's personal and professional relationships, leading to feelings of isolation and low self-esteem.

To determine if you have an inferiority or superiority complex, you can ask yourself the following questions:

<u>Inferiority Complex:</u>

Do I frequently compare myself to others and feel like I fall short?

Do I avoid taking risks or trying new things because I fear failure?

Do I seek validation and approval from others constantly?

Do I feel inadequate or inferior to others in various situations?

Superiority Complex:

Do I believe I am better or more talented than others?

Do I have a tendency to look down on others or belittle them?

Do I dominate conversations and relationships?

Do I feel a sense of entitlement or believe I deserve special treatment?

If you answered yes to many of the questions related to either complex, it might be worth considering seeking support from a mental health professional who can help you better understand and work through these feelings.

If you have an inferiority or superiority complex, here are some steps you can take to work through and overcome these feelings:

Inferiority Complex:

- ✓ Challenge your negative self-talk and beliefs. Try to identify when you are engaging in negative self-talk and replace it with positive affirmations and self-encouragement.
- ✓ Practice self-compassion and self-care. Treat yourself with kindness and understanding and

engage in activities that bring you joy and fulfilment.

- ✓ Focus on your strengths and accomplishments. Keep a record of your achievements and remind yourself of your strengths and positive qualities.
- ✓ Engage in personal growth opportunities. Try new things, take on challenges, and embrace new experiences to help build your confidence.

Superiority Complex:

- ✓ Practice empathy and humility. Try to understand the perspectives of others and acknowledge their strengths and achievements.
- ✓ Engage in activities that challenge your beliefs. Volunteer or work with people who have different experiences or perspectives to help broaden your outlook.
- ✓ Seek feedback and criticism. Ask for constructive feedback from others to help you understand your limitations and areas for growth.
- ✓ Reflect on your own insecurities. Consider the reasons behind your feelings of superiority and work on addressing any underlying insecurities or fears.

Overcoming these complexes takes time and effort, and seeking support from a mental health professional can be beneficial in managing these feelings.

Money is just an enabler

Money is often seen as the ultimate goal of success, but in reality, it is merely an enabler. It provides the means for people to achieve their goals and live their desired lifestyles. However, it is not the end in itself. In other words, money is a tool that can help people attain what they want, but it is not the only thing that brings happiness or fulfilment in life. In this chapter, I will explain how money is an enabler and provide some examples to support my argument.

To begin with, money can provide the means for people to achieve their goals. For instance, it can help people start their own businesses, pursue higher education, or travel to different parts of the world. Without money, these opportunities may not be available to everyone. Therefore, money can be seen as an enabler that unlocks potential and opens up new doors for people.

Furthermore, money can also provide people with the ability to support themselves and their families. This can lead to a sense of security and stability in life. Money can help people pay for their basic needs like food, shelter, and healthcare. Additionally, it can help them to provide for their families and give their loved ones a better life. Without money, people may struggle to provide for themselves and their families, leading to stress and anxiety.

It is essential to remember that money alone cannot bring happiness or fulfilment. It is merely a means to an end. People must use money to pursue their passions and live their desired lifestyles to achieve true satisfaction in life.

For example, a person with a high-paying job may have all the money in the world, but if they do not enjoy their work or find it meaningful, they may not feel fulfilled. On the other hand, a person with less money may find happiness by pursuing a career that aligns with their passions and values.

In conclusion, money is an enabler that can help people achieve their goals and provide for themselves and their families. It provides access to opportunities that may not be available to everyone. However, it is crucial to recognize that money alone cannot bring happiness or fulfilment in life. People must use it as a tool to pursue their passions and live their desired lifestyles to achieve true satisfaction in life. Therefore, it is important to prioritize one's goals and values, and use money as a means to an end rather than an end in itself.

Reading habits

Reading is a fundamental habit that has the potential to transform our lives. Reading has been proven to enhance our cognitive abilities, improve our communication skills, and expand our knowledge base. Daily reading habits help us to become successful by providing us with the tools we need to achieve our goals, enhancing our creativity, and improving our overall quality of life. In this chapter, we will explore how daily reading habits can help us to become successful.

Expanding Our Knowledge Base:

Reading helps us to acquire knowledge in a variety of areas. It helps us to learn about different cultures, histories, and ideas. This knowledge can be applied in a range of fields, including business, education, and personal development. By reading books, newspapers, and magazines, we become exposed to different perspectives, which can be a powerful tool for personal and professional growth.

Improving Our Vocabulary and Communication Skills:

Reading helps us to improve our vocabulary and communication skills. A broad vocabulary is essential for effective communication, and reading exposes us to new words and phrases, which we can incorporate into our daily conversations. Reading also helps us to develop our communication skills by exposing us to different writing styles, which we can emulate in our own writing and speaking. Good communication skills are critical for success in any field, and daily reading habits can help us to develop these skills.

Boosting Our Creativity:

Reading has been shown to boost creativity. By exposing ourselves to new ideas and concepts, we can develop fresh perspectives and new ideas. Reading also helps us to develop our imagination, which is critical for creative problem-solving. Daily reading habits can help us to think outside the box, and approach challenges with a more open mind, leading to innovative solutions and ideas.

Enhancing Our Critical Thinking Skills:

Reading is an excellent way to improve our critical thinking skills. By reading books and articles, we are exposed to different arguments and viewpoints. This exposure helps us to develop our critical thinking skills by challenging us to evaluate and analyse the information presented. Daily reading habits help us to develop our ability to think critically, which is essential for success in any field.

Building Our Confidence:

Daily reading habits can help us to build our confidence. By reading books and articles, we become more knowledgeable and well-informed. This knowledge can help us to approach challenges with a greater sense of confidence and clarity. Daily reading habits can also expose us to different perspectives, helping us to develop a more open-minded and confident approach to problem-solving.

Developing Our Focus and Concentration:

Reading requires focus and concentration, and daily reading habits can help us to develop these essential skills. By regularly setting aside time to read, we can improve our ability to concentrate and focus on tasks for extended periods. This focus and concentration are essential for success in any field, as they allow us to work efficiently and effectively towards our goals.

Reducing Stress and Improving Mental Health:

Daily reading habits can also help to reduce stress and improve mental health. Reading is a relaxing activity that can help us to unwind and escape from the stresses of daily life. It has been shown to reduce stress levels and improve overall mental health. By incorporating daily reading habits into our routines, we can enjoy the mental health benefits of this activity, leading to a more fulfilling and successful life.

Daily reading habits are essential for personal and professional success. Reading helps us to expand our knowledge base, improve our communication skills, boost our creativity, enhance our critical thinking skills, build our confidence, develop our focus and concentration, and improve our mental health. By incorporating daily reading habits into our routines, we can enjoy the numerous benefits of this activity, leading to a more fulfilling and successful life.

Cryptocurrency

Cryptocurrency, a digital currency that is secured by cryptography and operates independently of a central bank, has emerged as a major technological and financial innovation in recent years. At its core, cryptocurrency is a decentralized system that allows for peer-to-peer transactions, without the need for intermediaries such as banks or government agencies. Cryptocurrency has been hailed by many as a revolutionary concept that has the potential to transform the global financial system. However, it is also a complex and sometimes controversial topic, with many questions remaining about its long-term viability and impact on society.

At its most basic level, cryptocurrency is a digital asset that is designed to function as a medium of exchange. It is created and secured using advanced encryption techniques, which allow for secure and anonymous transactions. Unlike traditional currency, which is issued and regulated by central banks, cryptocurrency is decentralized, meaning that it is not controlled by any government or financial institution. This means that cryptocurrency can be used for transactions across borders, without the need for intermediaries such as banks or other financial institutions.

One of the key features of cryptocurrency is its use of a blockchain, a decentralized ledger that records all transactions in a transparent and secure manner. Each transaction is recorded as a block, which is then added to the blockchain in a sequential order. This makes it very difficult for anyone to alter or manipulate the blockchain, as it would require them to rewrite the entire history of the chain. This creates a high level of security and transparency, making cryptocurrency a very attractive option for those who value privacy and security in their financial transactions.

There are many different types of cryptocurrencies, each with its own unique features and characteristics. The most well-known cryptocurrency is Bitcoin, which was created in 2009 by an unknown person or group using the pseudonym Satoshi Nakamoto. Bitcoin was designed to be a decentralized and secure currency that could be used for transactions across borders without the need for intermediaries. Since its creation, Bitcoin has become a global phenomenon, with millions of people around the world using it for transactions of all kinds.

Other cryptocurrencies have emerged in recent years, including Ethereum, Litecoin, and Ripple. Each of these cryptocurrencies has its own unique features and uses, but they all share the common characteristic of being decentralized and secure. Ethereum, for example, is designed to be a platform for building decentralized applications, while Litecoin is designed to be a faster and more efficient version of Bitcoin.

Despite the many benefits of cryptocurrency, there are also some significant challenges and controversies surrounding this emerging technology. One of the biggest concerns is the potential for criminal activity, as cryptocurrency has been used in some cases to facilitate illegal transactions such as drug trafficking and money laundering. However, it is important to note that cryptocurrency is not inherently illegal or immoral, and that it can be used for many legitimate purposes as well.

Another concern is the volatility of cryptocurrency markets, which can be highly unpredictable and subject to sudden changes. This can make it difficult for investors to know when to buy or sell, and can create significant risks for those who invest in this technology. However, as the cryptocurrency market matures and stabilizes, it is expected that volatility will decrease and the market will become more predictable.

Finally, there are concerns about the long-term viability of cryptocurrency as a global currency. While many people believe that cryptocurrency has the potential to revolutionize the global financial system, others are sceptical that it will ever be widely adopted as a mainstream currency. This is due in part to the fact that cryptocurrency is still relatively new and untested, and there are many challenges and hurdles that must be overcome before it can achieve widespread acceptance.

Whether or not a common person should invest in cryptocurrency is a complex question that ultimately depends on a variety of factors, including their financial goals, risk tolerance, and understanding of the cryptocurrency market.

On the one hand, cryptocurrency has the potential to provide significant returns on investment, especially given the high levels of volatility and price fluctuations in the market. Some people have made significant amounts of money through their investments in cryptocurrency, particularly those who invested early in the market and held onto their investments as the market grew.

On the other hand, investing in cryptocurrency can be very risky, particularly for those who are not familiar with the market or do not have a solid understanding of the technology behind cryptocurrency. The market can be highly unpredictable, with prices fluctuating rapidly and often without warning. There have also been many cases of fraud and scams in the cryptocurrency market, which can result in significant financial losses for investors.

Before investing in cryptocurrency, it is important for individuals to carefully evaluate their financial goals and risk tolerance. They should also take the time to research the cryptocurrency market and gain a solid understanding of the technology and its potential risks and benefits. It is also important to keep in mind that cryptocurrency should be considered a high-risk investment, and that individuals should never invest more than they can afford to lose.

History of Taxation

Taxation has played a significant role in human history, with governments and rulers throughout time using taxes as a means of generating revenue to fund their activities and maintain power. The history of taxation can be traced back thousands of years, with examples of taxation systems dating as far back as ancient civilizations such as Egypt, Greece, and Rome.

The earliest known taxation system dates back to ancient Egypt, where tax collectors were responsible for collecting taxes on crops, livestock, and other resources. The Pharaohs used these taxes to fund their military campaigns and to build public works projects such as temples and irrigation systems. In ancient Greece, taxes were also used to fund the military and public works projects, with taxes collected in the form of coins, livestock, and other goods.

During the Roman Empire, taxes played a crucial role in the maintenance of the vast empire. The Roman government levied a wide range of taxes, including property taxes, sales taxes, and taxes on imported goods. The Roman tax system was highly complex and involved a vast bureaucracy of tax collectors and assessors. However, the high levels of taxation, along with other factors such as corruption and military defeats, contributed to the decline and eventual collapse of the Roman Empire.

During the Middle Ages, taxation continued to be a major source of revenue for governments. In Europe, feudal lords and monarchs levied taxes on their subjects in the form of land rents, tribute payments, and other goods. The Catholic Church also levied taxes, with tithes collected from the faithful to fund the Church's activities.

In the 16th century, the rise of nation-states in Europe led to the development of more centralized taxation systems. The first income tax was introduced in Britain in 1799, as a means of financing the Napoleonic Wars. The tax was levied on incomes above a certain threshold and was based on a percentage of the individual's income. Other European countries soon followed suit, and by the early 20th century, income taxes had become a standard part of the tax systems of most developed countries.

In the United States, taxes played a significant role in the country's founding and development. In the years leading up to the American Revolution, colonists protested against British taxes such as the Stamp Act and the Tea Act, arguing that they were being unfairly taxed without representation in the British Parliament. This led to the famous slogan "no taxation without representation," and ultimately to the American Revolution.

After the Revolutionary War, the new American government was faced with the challenge of funding its activities without the support of British taxes. The government levied taxes on imported goods and other items, and in 1862, the first income tax was introduced in the United States to fund the Civil War. The tax was later abolished, but was reintroduced in 1913 with the ratification of the 16th Amendment to the U.S. Constitution.

In the 20th century, taxation played a major role in the development of the welfare state and the expansion of social programs in many countries. Governments used taxes to fund programs such as healthcare, education, and social security, with the goal of reducing poverty and promoting greater equality. However, taxes have also been the subject of much controversy and debate, with critics arguing that high tax rates can stifle economic growth and discourage innovation.

Today, taxation continues to play a crucial role in the functioning of modern societies. Governments rely on taxes to fund a wide range of activities, from infrastructure development to national defence to social programs. However, debates continue about the best ways to structure tax systems to ensure fairness and promote economic growth, while also addressing issues such as income inequality and the impact of globalization on tax revenues.

Taxation has a long and complex history in India, dating back to ancient times. The earliest recorded tax system in India is from the Indus Valley Civilization, which existed around 2,500 BCE. The civilization's taxation system was primarily based on the collection of agricultural produce, such as grain, cotton, and wool.

During the Mauryan Empire (321-185 BCE), the first centralized taxation system was introduced in India. The emperor Chandragupta Maurya established a system of revenue collection known as the bali system, which involved the collection of one-sixth of the agricultural produce as tax. The system was later refined by the emperor Ashoka, who established a network of officials and accountants to ensure efficient and fair collection of taxes.

During the Mughal Empire (1526-1857), a sophisticated tax system was developed that was based on land revenue. The Mughals levied a tax known as the zamin-dari system, which involved the collection of a fixed percentage of the agricultural produce as land revenue. The system was based on the idea that the state was the ultimate owner of the land, and that individuals were granted the right to use the land in exchange for payment of taxes.

During British colonial rule in India (1757-1947), the taxation system was significantly expanded and restructured to suit the needs of the colonial administration. The British introduced a range of new taxes, including income tax, customs duties, and excise taxes, which were designed to generate revenue for the colonial government.

After India gained independence in 1947, the taxation system was reformed and expanded to support the needs of the new democratic government. The Constitution of India provided for a federal system of taxation, with the power to levy taxes shared between the central and state governments. The tax system was based on a variety of taxes, including income tax, sales tax, excise tax, customs duties, and service tax.

Today, the taxation system in India is complex and multifaceted, with a wide range of taxes levied by both the central and state governments. The system is designed to generate revenue to support the needs of the government, including infrastructure development, social programs, and national defence. The tax system is also designed to be fair and equitable, with progressive tax rates and exemptions for low-income earners.

Why gold is costly?

Gold has been valued for thousands of years, and is considered one of the most valuable and sought-after metals in the world. There are a number of factors that contribute to the high cost of gold, including its rarity, physical properties, and cultural significance.

One of the main reasons gold is so costly is its rarity. Gold is a relatively rare element in the earth's crust, and is typically found in small concentrations in ores and alluvial deposits. This means that large amounts of rock and soil must be mined and processed in order to extract a small amount of gold. In addition, gold deposits are often located in remote or difficult-to-access areas, which makes mining and processing more expensive.

Another factor that contributes to the high cost of gold is its physical properties. Gold is a dense, malleable metal that is highly resistant to corrosion and tarnishing. These properties make it ideal for use in jewellery and other decorative objects, as well as in a variety of industrial applications. However, the properties that make gold so useful also make it more difficult to mine and process, which contributes to its high cost.

Cultural significance is also a factor in the high cost of gold. Gold has been valued by many cultures throughout history, and is often associated with wealth, power, and status. In many societies, gold is used as a form of currency or as a store of value, and is often exchanged as a symbol of prestige or as a means of settling debts. This cultural significance has helped to create a strong demand for gold, which in turn drives up its price.

Finally, the price of gold is also influenced by a variety of economic and political factors. Because gold is often seen as a safe-haven investment, its price may rise during times of economic or political uncertainty. Similarly, the price of gold may fall during periods of economic growth or stability, as investors seek out riskier, higher-yielding investments.

Overall, the high cost of gold is the result of a complex interplay between physical properties, rarity, cultural significance, and economic and political factors. While the cost of gold may fluctuate over time, its enduring value and appeal ensure that it will remain a sought-after and valuable commodity for generations to come.

The price of gold is determined by a complex set of factors, including supply and demand, economic indicators, geopolitical events, and the actions of various financial institutions and central banks. While no single entity controls the price of gold, there are several key players that can influence it in various ways.

One of the main drivers of the price of gold is the demand for it in the global market. Gold is often seen as a safe-haven asset, particularly during times of economic or political uncertainty. When investors become concerned about the stability of traditional investments such as stocks and bonds, they may turn to gold as a way to protect their wealth. This increased demand can drive up the price of gold.

Another factor that can influence the price of gold is the supply of it in the market. Gold is a finite resource, and the cost of mining and refining it can be expensive.

Changes in mining practices or shifts in global production can impact the supply of gold and thereby affect its price.

Central banks and financial institutions also play a role in determining the price of gold. Central banks hold significant amounts of gold as part of their foreign currency reserves, and their actions regarding buying and selling gold can affect its price. Similarly, large financial institutions may hold significant positions in gold, and their trading activity can impact its price.

Geopolitical events and economic indicators can also influence the price of gold. For example, tensions between major global powers or the outbreak of a global pandemic can increase demand for gold as a safe-haven asset, while positive economic news such as strong job growth or higher interest rates can decrease demand for gold.

Importance of having a hobby

Having a hobby is important for a variety of reasons, both for personal fulfilment and for overall well-being. Here are some reasons why having a hobby is important, along with examples of hobbies that people may enjoy:

Reduce stress and improve mental health: Hobbies can provide an outlet for stress and anxiety, as well as improve overall mental health. Hobbies such as meditation, yoga, painting, or gardening can be great for reducing stress and promoting relaxation.

Promote creativity: Hobbies allow people to tap into their creative side, whether it is through writing, drawing, or music. Engaging in creative activities can help to boost creativity and provide a sense of accomplishment.

Develop new skills: Hobbies can help people learn new skills and gain knowledge in a variety of areas. Hobbies such as cooking, woodworking, or learning a new language can be great for expanding knowledge and developing new skills.

Build social connections: Hobbies can be a great way to connect with others who share similar interests. Whether it's through a local sports team, a book club, or a crafting group, hobbies can provide opportunities for socializing and building connections with others.

Increase physical activity: Hobbies can be a fun way to stay active and healthy. Activities such as hiking, biking, or playing a sport can be great for physical fitness and overall well-being.

Some examples of popular hobbies include:

Reading: Whether it's fiction, non-fiction, or poetry, reading can be a great way to escape and expand knowledge.

Cooking: Cooking can be a fun way to experiment with new flavours and ingredients, as well as to nourish oneself and others.

Photography: Photography can be a creative outlet and a way to capture memories and moments.

Playing a musical instrument: Playing a musical instrument can be a great way to express oneself creatively and connect with others through music.

Gardening: Gardening can be a peaceful and relaxing hobby, as well as a way to connect with nature and grow one's own food.

Having a hobby can be beneficial for overall well-being and personal fulfilment. Hobbies can reduce stress, promote creativity, develop new skills, build social connections, and increase physical activity. There are many different hobbies to choose from, and it's important to find one that fits one's interests and lifestyle. By making time for a hobby, people can enjoy the benefits of personal growth, fulfilment, and overall well-being.

Unknown facts about human brain

The human brain is one of the most complex and fascinating organs in the body, and there are many unknown facts about its capabilities and functions. Here are some examples of lesser-known facts about the human brain:

The brain is capable of rewiring itself: This ability is known as neuroplasticity and means that the brain can adapt to new experiences and learn new skills. For example, studies have shown that learning a new language can increase the size of certain areas of the brain.

The brain can create false memories: Studies have shown that the brain can be tricked into creating false memories, which can be as vivid and detailed as real memories. For example, a person may remember an event that never actually happened.

The brain consumes a lot of energy: Although the brain represents only about 2% of the body's weight, it uses about 20% of the body's energy. This is because the brain is constantly working to process information and regulate bodily functions.

The brain can process information faster than a computer: While computers can perform complex calculations at lightning speed, the human brain is still faster at processing certain types of information, such as recognizing faces or processing emotions.

The brain can change its own structure in response to mental training: Studies have shown that activities such as meditation and mindfulness can lead to changes in the structure of the brain, including increased grey matter and changes in the activity of certain brain regions.

The brain can create its own painkillers: The brain can produce endorphins, which are natural painkillers that can help to reduce pain and promote feelings of well-being. Endorphins are released during activities such as exercise and laughter.

The human brain is an incredibly complex and fascinating organ that is still not fully understood. These lesser-known facts about the brain demonstrate its incredible capabilities and highlight the importance of continued research and exploration.

Human dreams

Dreaming is a natural and essential part of the sleep cycle. While we sleep, our brains are still active, and we experience a wide range of cognitive and emotional processes, including dreaming. Although the exact function of dreaming is still not fully understood, scientists have made significant progress in understanding the science behind human night dreams.

The brain is divided into different regions, including the frontal cortex, limbic system, and brainstem, each of which plays a role in the dreaming process. During the early stages of sleep, the brain moves from the waking state to a relaxed and receptive state, allowing for the occurrence of dreaming.

One of the most important factors in the dreaming process is rapid eye movement (REM) sleep, which occurs several times throughout the night. During REM sleep, the body becomes immobilized, while the brain is highly active, and the eyes move rapidly back and forth. It is during this stage of sleep that most vivid and memorable dreams occur.

The content of dreams is thought to be related to the individual's current concerns, experiences, and emotions. Dreams may reflect recent events or long-term memories, and can often incorporate elements of the individual's fears, hopes, and aspirations. Dreams may also help to consolidate and process emotional experiences, allowing individuals to better regulate their emotions and cope with stress.

The exact neural mechanisms behind dreaming are still not fully understood, but several theories have been proposed. One theory suggests that the frontal cortex is responsible for generating dreams, while another theory proposes that the limbic system, which is involved in emotion and memory, plays a more significant role.

Despite the progress that has been made in understanding the science behind dreaming, there is still much we do not know about this complex and fascinating process. Ongoing research is essential to further our understanding of the neural mechanisms behind dreaming, and to explore the potential functions and benefits of this important aspect of the sleep cycle.

In conclusion, dreaming is a natural and essential part of the human experience, occurring during the sleep cycle as a result of complex neural processes in the brain. While the exact function of dreaming is still not fully understood, continued research is essential to further our understanding of this fascinating and mysterious phenomenon.

<u>There is a connection between our thoughts and night dreams.</u> The content of our dreams is often influenced by our waking thoughts and experiences. During the day, we encounter various situations and stimuli that can be incorporated into our dreams at night. For example, if we experience a stressful event during the day, we may have a dream that reflects that stress.

Our thoughts and emotions can influence the tone and content of our dreams. For instance, if we are feeling anxious or afraid, we may have a nightmare, while if we are feeling happy or content, we may have a pleasant dream. Some research suggests that our dreams can help us to process and consolidate emotional experiences from our waking lives. Dreams may serve as a form of emotional regulation, helping us to cope with stress and process challenging experiences. In this sense, our thoughts and emotions during the day may influence the content of our dreams, while our dreams may, in turn, influence our thoughts and emotions during waking life.

Finally, we can say, there is a connection between our thoughts and night dreams, as the content of our dreams is often influenced by our waking thoughts and experiences. Our dreams may also help us to process and regulate our emotions, and may influence our thoughts and feelings during the day.

Night dreams can be a rich source of information about our innermost thoughts, emotions, and desires. Dreams can provide insights into our subconscious minds, allowing us to better understand ourselves and our experiences. Therefore, it is generally beneficial to pay attention to our dreams and to try to interpret their meanings.

While not all dreams may be meaningful or relevant to our waking lives, many dreams can offer important insights into our emotional states and experiences. Dreams can help us to process and cope with difficult emotions and experiences, and may provide creative solutions to real-world problems.

However, it is important to approach dream interpretation with a degree of scepticism and critical thinking. Not all dream interpretations are accurate or relevant, and it is important to consider the broader context of our waking lives when interpreting our dreams.

Some people may benefit from keeping a dream journal or seeking the help of a therapist or dream interpreter to better understand the meaning of their dreams. However, for others, simply reflecting on their dreams and considering their emotional and symbolic content may be enough to gain insights and understanding.

In conclusion, while not all night dreams may be significant or relevant, paying attention to our dreams can offer valuable insights into our inner world and help us to better understand ourselves and our experiences. By interpreting our dreams with a critical eye and considering the broader context of our waking lives, we can gain a deeper understanding of ourselves and our emotional experiences.

Interpreting night dreams can be a complex and multifaceted process that involves considering the various symbols and themes present in the dream, as well as the emotions and experiences of the dreamer. While dream interpretation is not an exact science, there are several approaches and techniques that can be used to better understand the meaning of a dream.

One common approach to dream interpretation is to consider the symbolic meaning of the various elements present in the dream. For example, many people believe that certain symbols, such as snakes or water, have particular meanings and associations. By examining the various symbols present in a dream and considering their potential meanings, we can gain insights into the emotional and psychological themes present in the dream.

Another approach to dream interpretation is to consider the emotional content of the dream. Dreams can be highly emotional experiences, and by examining the feelings and emotions present in a dream, we can gain insights into our inner world and our psychological state. For example, a dream that is characterized by fear or anxiety may reflect a sense of insecurity or vulnerability in our waking lives.

Finally, it is important to consider the context of the dream when interpreting its meaning. Dreams can be influenced by a wide range of factors, including our current experiences, memories, and beliefs. By considering the broader context of our waking lives, we can gain a better understanding of the potential meaning of a dream.

One historical example of the interpretation of dreams is found in the biblical story of Joseph and the Pharaoh. According to the story, Pharaoh had a dream that he could not interpret, and he sought the help of Joseph, who was known for his ability to interpret dreams. Joseph interpreted Pharaoh's dream as a warning of an impending famine, and he advised Pharaoh to store up food in preparation. This interpretation helped to save the people of Egypt from starvation.

Another historical example of dream interpretation is found in the work of Carl Jung, who believed that dreams were a reflection of the collective unconscious, or the shared experiences and archetypes of humanity. Jung developed a system of dream interpretation that involved analysing the various symbols and themes present in the dream, as well as considering the personal and collective associations of these symbols. Jung believed that dreams could offer insights into the deeper, unconscious aspects of the psyche, and that by interpreting dreams, individuals could gain a greater understanding of their inner world and their place in the world.

Interpreting night dreams involves considering the symbolic meaning of the various elements present in the dream, as well as the emotions and experiences of the dreamer. By examining the broader context of the dream and considering its potential meaning, we can gain insights into our inner world and our psychological state. While dream interpretation is not an exact science, it can be a valuable tool for gaining a deeper understanding of ourselves and our experiences.

Having a Guru

In many cultures and traditions, the concept of having a guru or a spiritual teacher is considered to be of great importance. A guru is someone who has attained a high level of spiritual realization and can guide others on their own spiritual path. The philosophy of having a guru in life is based on the idea that spiritual growth and enlightenment are not something that can be achieved solely through personal effort or intellectual understanding. Rather, they require the guidance and wisdom of someone who has already walked the path.

The role of a guru is to serve as a spiritual guide and mentor, helping the disciple to deepen their understanding of spiritual principles and to overcome obstacles on the path. The relationship between a guru and disciple is often seen as a sacred bond, based on trust, devotion, and a deep mutual respect. The disciple looks to the guru for guidance, support, and inspiration, while the guru provides teachings, practices, and insights to help the disciple progress on their spiritual journey.

The philosophy of having a guru in life is based on the belief that spiritual growth is not a linear process, but rather a series of cycles and stages that require guidance and support. The guru is seen as a catalyst for this growth, helping the disciple to uncover their true nature and to cultivate the qualities of love, compassion, and wisdom. Through the teachings and practices of the guru, the disciple is able to develop a deeper awareness of their own inner world and to connect with the divine source of all creation.

While the concept of having a guru is often associated with Eastern traditions such as Hinduism, Buddhism, and Sikhism, it is also present in many other spiritual traditions and practices around the world. In Western spiritual traditions, the concept of having a spiritual director or mentor is similar to that of having a guru.

In conclusion, the philosophy of having a guru in life is based on the idea that spiritual growth and enlightenment are not something that can be achieved solely through personal effort or intellectual understanding. Rather, they require the guidance and wisdom of someone who has already walked the path. The role of a guru is to serve as a spiritual guide and mentor, helping the disciple to deepen their understanding of spiritual principles and to overcome obstacles on the path. Through the teachings and practices of the guru, the disciple is able to develop a deeper awareness of their own inner world and to connect with the divine source of all creation.

The decision to seek a guru or spiritual teacher is a deeply personal one, and there is no one-size-fits-all answer to this question. However, there are some signs that may indicate that you could benefit from the guidance of a guru. Here are some things to consider:

Feeling stuck or lost on your spiritual path: If you have been practicing spiritual disciplines for some time and feel like you are not making progress or are unsure of what to do next, a guru may be able to provide guidance and support.

Seeking deeper understanding: If you have a deep yearning for spiritual growth and want to deepen your understanding of spiritual principles, a guru can provide teachings and practices to help you do so.

Experiencing a spiritual crisis: If you are going through a challenging time and are struggling with questions of purpose and meaning, a guru can offer spiritual guidance and help you navigate these difficult times.

Desire for a deeper connection to the divine: If you are seeking a deeper connection to the divine and want to cultivate a more meaningful relationship with the divine, a guru can offer practices and teachings to help you do so.

Openness to the guru-disciple relationship: If you are open to the idea of having a guru and are willing to submit to their guidance, a guru may be a good fit for you.

It is important to note that seeking a guru should not be taken lightly and should be done with care and discernment. It is important to research potential gurus and make sure that their teachings and practices are in alignment with your own values and beliefs. It is also important to approach the relationship with humility and openness, as the guru-disciple relationship is a deeply personal and transformative one.

The decision to seek a guru or spiritual teacher is a personal one, and there are no hard and fast rules about who needs one. However, if you are feeling stuck on your spiritual path, seeking deeper understanding, experiencing a spiritual crisis, desiring a deeper connection to the divine, and are open to the guru-disciple relationship, seeking the guidance of a guru may be a good fit for you.

Breathing techniques to calm the mind

Breathing techniques are a simple and effective way to calm the mind and reduce stress and anxiety. Here are some breathing techniques that can be helpful in calming the mind:

Diaphragmatic Breathing:

Diaphragmatic breathing, also known as deep breathing or belly breathing, involves inhaling deeply through the nose, filling up the lungs and expanding the belly, and then exhaling slowly through the mouth. This type of breathing helps to slow down the heart rate, reduce stress hormones, and increase feelings of relaxation and calm.

Here are the steps for diaphragmatic breathing:

Find a comfortable position, either sitting or lying down, with your back straight.

Place one hand on your chest and the other hand on your belly.

Take a deep breath in through your nose, filling up your lungs and expanding your belly.

Exhale slowly through your mouth, letting your belly fall inward.

Repeat this pattern for several minutes, focusing on the sensation of your belly rising and falling with each breath.

Alternate Nostril Breathing:

Alternate nostril breathing is a technique that involves alternating the flow of air through each nostril. This technique helps to balance the flow of energy in the body, and promote feelings of calm and relaxation.

Here are the steps for alternate nostril breathing:

Find a comfortable seated position, with your back straight.

Place your right thumb on your right nostril, and your right ring finger on your left nostril.

Close your right nostril with your thumb, and inhale deeply through your left nostril.

Close your left nostril with your ring finger, and hold your breath for a few seconds.

Release your thumb and exhale through your right nostril.

Inhale through your right nostril, then close it with your thumb and hold your breath for a few seconds.

Release your ring finger and exhale through your left nostril.

Repeat this pattern for several minutes, alternating nostrils with each inhale and exhale.

Box Breathing:

Box breathing, also known as square breathing, is a technique that involves inhaling for a count of four, holding the breath for a count of four, exhaling for a count of four, and holding the breath for a count of four. This type of breathing helps to regulate the nervous system, slow the heart rate, and promote feelings of calm and relaxation.

Here are the steps for box breathing:

Find a comfortable seated position, with your back straight.

Inhale through your nose for a count of four.

Hold your breath for a count of four.

Exhale through your mouth for a count of four.

Hold your breath for a count of four.

Repeat this pattern for several minutes, focusing on the sensation of your breath moving in and out of your body.

4-7-8 Breathing:

The 4-7-8 breathing technique involves inhaling through the nose for a count of four, holding the breath for a count of seven, and exhaling through the mouth for a count of eight. This type of breathing helps to reduce stress and anxiety, and promote feelings of calm and relaxation.

Here are the steps for 4-7-8 breathing:

Find a comfortable seated position, with your back straight.

Inhale through your nose for a count of four.

Hold your breath for a count of seven.

Exhale through your mouth for a count of eight.

Repeat this pattern for several minutes, focusing on the sensation of your breath moving in and out of your body.

Overall, these breathing techniques can be helpful in calming the mind, reducing stress and anxiety, and promoting feelings of relaxation and well-being.

Mobile games

Mobile gaming has become a popular form of entertainment in India, with a growing number of players and a thriving gaming industry. Here are some statistics on mobile game players in India:

India is the second-largest market for mobile gaming in the world, with an estimated 405 million mobile gamers in the country.

The mobile gaming industry in India is expected to grow to $1.1 billion by 2020, up from $290 million in 2016.

The average age of mobile gamers in India is 28 years old, and 84% of mobile gamers in India are under the age of 35.

The majority of mobile gamers in India are male, with 71% of mobile gamers in the country being male and 29% being female.

The most popular genres of mobile games in India are action, adventure, and racing games, followed by puzzle and strategy games.

The average time spent playing mobile games in India is around 60 minutes per day, with around 89% of mobile gamers in the country playing games every day.

The top mobile games in India include games like PubG Mobile, Ludo King, Candy Crush Saga, and Clash of Clans.

These statistics demonstrate the growing popularity of mobile gaming in India, as well as the significant potential for growth in the industry.

Mobile games are designed to be addictive because addiction is good for business. Game developers create games that are engaging, motivating, and rewarding, with the goal of keeping players playing for as long as possible. Some of the key reasons why mobile games are addictive include:

Rewards: Mobile games are designed to provide rewards to players for completing tasks, achieving goals, or reaching new levels. These rewards can be in the form of points, virtual currency, or other items that can be used to enhance the player's experience or progress further in the game. The feeling of accomplishment that comes with these rewards can be addictive, as players are motivated to continue playing to earn more rewards.

Progression: Mobile games are often designed to provide a sense of progression, with players gradually unlocking new features, challenges, and rewards as they play. This sense of progression can be addictive, as players are motivated to continue playing in order to see what comes next.

Social Interaction: Many mobile games include social features, such as leader boards, chat, and the ability to play with friends. These social interactions can be addictive, as players are motivated to compete with others, form alliances, or collaborate in order to achieve success in the game.

Instant Gratification: Mobile games are often designed to provide instant gratification, with players receiving rewards or feedback immediately for their actions in the game. This can be addictive, as players are conditioned to expect instant results and may find it difficult to resist the urge to keep playing for just one more level or reward.

Psychological Triggers: Mobile games can be designed to trigger certain psychological responses in players, such as excitement, anticipation, or a sense of accomplishment. These psychological triggers can be addictive, as players become conditioned to associate the game with positive feelings and are motivated to continue playing in order to experience those feelings again.

Overall, mobile games are designed to be addictive by providing a sense of accomplishment, progression, and social interaction, as well as by triggering certain psychological responses in players. While mobile games can be a source of entertainment and enjoyment, it is important for individuals to be aware of the potential addictive nature of these games and to practice moderation and self-control when playing.

While mobile games can be a fun form of entertainment, they can also have negative impacts on society in some cases. Here are some ways in which mobile games can be damaging to our society:

Addiction: Mobile games can be highly addictive, leading to excessive use and potentially harmful consequences, such as neglecting work or school, social isolation, and health problems.

Distraction: Mobile games can distract people from important tasks, such as driving, working, or studying, which can lead to accidents or decreased productivity.

Social isolation: Mobile games can contribute to social isolation, as players may spend more time interacting with their devices than with other people, leading to a decrease in social skills and real-life interactions.

Negative impact on mental health: Excessive mobile game use has been linked to mental health issues, such as depression and anxiety, especially in vulnerable populations such as children and teenagers.

Exposure to inappropriate content: Some mobile games feature violent or sexual content, which can be inappropriate for younger players.

Promoting unhealthy habits: Some mobile games encourage unhealthy behaviours, such as spending money on in-app purchases or promoting sedentary lifestyles.

Sleep disruption: Mobile games can interfere with sleep patterns, as players may stay up late or wake up early to play games.

These negative impacts on society demonstrate the importance of using mobile games in moderation and being mindful of their potential consequences.

Cyber Attracts

A cyber-attack is a malicious attempt to disrupt, damage, or gain unauthorized access to a computer system, network, or device. Cyber-attacks can take many forms, and can range from simple attacks like phishing emails to complex attacks like distributed denial-of-service (DDoS) attacks or malware infections.

Cyber-attacks are becoming more common and more sophisticated, and can have a wide range of impacts, including:

Financial losses: Cyber-attacks can result in financial losses, both for individuals and for businesses, due to stolen data or funds, or costs associated with repairing damage to systems.

Privacy violations: Cyber-attacks can lead to the theft or exposure of sensitive personal or financial information, which can be used for identity theft or other malicious purposes.

System downtime: Some cyber-attacks can cause system downtime, preventing individuals or businesses from accessing important data or services.

Reputation damage: Cyber-attacks can damage the reputation of individuals or businesses, as well as erode trust in online systems and services.

National security risks: Some cyber-attacks can pose a threat to national security, such as attacks on critical infrastructure or government systems.

There are many different types of cyber-attacks, including phishing attacks, malware infections, denial-of-service attacks, ransomware attacks, and more. As technology continues to evolve, it is important to be aware of potential cyber threats and take steps to protect against them.

Phishing attacks: Phishing attacks are typically emails or other messages that are designed to trick people into revealing sensitive information or clicking on malicious links. These attacks can be highly effective, and can lead to data theft or malware infections.

Malware attacks: Malware is any software that is designed to harm or infiltrate a computer system or network. Malware can take many forms, including viruses, trojans, and ransomware.

Denial-of-service (DoS) attacks: DoS attacks are designed to overwhelm a website or network with traffic, making it impossible for legitimate users to access it. These attacks can be used for extortion, political activism, or other purposes.

Man-in-the-middle (MitM) attacks: MitM attacks are designed to intercept and modify data that is being transmitted between two parties. These attacks can be used to steal sensitive data or to inject malicious code into a system.

SQL injection attacks: SQL injection attacks are designed to exploit vulnerabilities in web applications that allow attackers to inject malicious code into a database. These attacks can be used to steal sensitive data or to gain control of a system.

Cross-site scripting (XSS) attacks: XSS attacks are similar to SQL injection attacks, but they exploit vulnerabilities in web applications that allow attackers to inject malicious code into a web page. These attacks can be used to steal sensitive data or to hijack user sessions.

Social engineering attacks: Social engineering attacks are designed to trick people into revealing sensitive information or performing actions that benefit the attacker. These attacks can take many forms, including phishing attacks, pretexting, and baiting.

These are just a few of the many types of cyber-attacks that exist. As technology continues to evolve, it is important to stay vigilant and take steps to protect against cyber threats.

There are several steps you can take to protect yourself from cyber-attacks. Here are some examples:

Keep your software up to date: Software vulnerabilities can be exploited by attackers, so it is important to keep your software up to date with the latest security patches. This includes your operating system, web browser, and any other software that you use regularly.

Use strong, unique passwords: Using strong, unique passwords for each of your accounts can help prevent attackers from accessing your accounts even if they obtain one password. Consider using a password manager to help you create and manage strong passwords.

Be cautious of suspicious emails and messages: Phishing attacks are a common way that attackers try to trick people into revealing sensitive information or clicking on malicious links. Be wary of any messages that ask for personal or financial information, or that contain suspicious links or attachments.

Use antivirus software: Antivirus software can help detect and prevent malware infections on your computer or device. Make sure to keep your antivirus software up to date with the latest security definitions.

Use two-factor authentication: Two-factor authentication adds an extra layer of security to your accounts by requiring you to enter a code in addition to your password. This can help prevent attackers from accessing your accounts even if they obtain your password.

Use a virtual private network (VPN): A VPN can help protect your internet traffic from prying eyes by encrypting it and routing it through a secure server. This can be especially useful when using public Wi-Fi networks, which are often not secure.

Back up your data: Backing up your important data can help protect you from data loss in the event of a malware infection or other cyber-attack. Make sure to keep your backups up to date and stored in a secure location.

By taking these steps and remaining vigilant, you can help protect yourself from cyber-attacks and keep your personal and financial information safe.

The first computer virus, known as "The Creeper", was created in the early 1970s by Bob Thomas, a programmer working on the ARPANET (Advanced Research Projects Agency Network), a precursor to the internet. The Creeper was not intended to be a harmful virus, but rather a test of whether it was possible to create self-replicating code.

The Creeper virus would travel between computers on the ARPANET and display the message "I'm the creeper, catch me if you can!" on the computer screen before moving on to the next computer. This led to the creation of the first antivirus software, known as "Reaper", which was designed to track down and remove the Creeper virus.

While the Creeper virus did not cause any significant damage or harm, it marked the beginning of the era of computer viruses and cyber-attacks. Since then, cyber-attacks have become increasingly sophisticated and widespread, with attackers using a variety of techniques to compromise computer systems, steal data, and cause damage.

How Antivirus software works?

Antivirus software works by scanning your computer or device for known viruses and other malicious software, and removing them if they are found. Here are the basic steps involved in how antivirus software works:

Signature detection: Antivirus software uses a database of known virus signatures to scan files on your computer or device. These signatures are unique code patterns that are associated with known viruses and malware.

Heuristic detection: Antivirus software can also use heuristic detection, which involves looking for suspicious behaviour that may be indicative of a new or unknown virus. For example, the software may look for code that tries to modify system files, or attempts to communicate with known malicious websites.

Behaviour-based detection: Some antivirus software can also use behaviour-based detection, which involves monitoring the behaviour of programs and looking for activity that is characteristic of malware. For example, the software may look for programs that try to access sensitive areas of the operating system, or that try to inject code into other programs.

Quarantine or remove infected files: If the antivirus software detects a virus or other malware, it will typically quarantine the infected files to prevent them from causing further damage. In some cases, the software may be able to remove the malware entirely.

Updates and scans: Antivirus software should be regularly updated with the latest virus definitions to ensure that it is able to detect the most recent threats. It is also important to regularly run scans of your computer or device to check for any new infections.

While antivirus software can help protect your computer or device from known viruses and malware, it is not fool proof and may not be able to detect all types of threats. It is important to practice good computer hygiene, such as avoiding suspicious websites and downloads, using strong passwords, and keeping your software up to date, in order to help prevent infections in the first place.

Building a large professional network

Building a large professional network is very important if you want to have a successful career over a long period of time. Here are a few reasons why:

Opportunities: Having a large professional network can help you discover new job opportunities that you may not have known about otherwise. Your network can inform you about openings at their companies or even refer you to job openings that fit your skills and experience.

Knowledge sharing: Having a diverse professional network can provide you with access to a wide range of knowledge and experience. You can learn from others' experiences and apply that knowledge to your own work, which can help you grow professionally.

Industry trends: By staying in touch with your professional network, you can stay up-to-date with the latest industry trends, which can help you stay ahead of the curve and make better decisions in your career.

Support: Building a strong network can also provide you with emotional support, particularly during challenging times in your career. You can turn to your network for advice and guidance, which can help you navigate difficult situations.

For example, let's say you are a software engineer who wants to work for your entire life. You attend industry events, participate in online forums, and connect with others in your field. As a result, you build a large network of contacts who share your interests and can offer advice, support, and guidance. One day, you learn about a new job opening from one of your contacts that matches your skills and interests perfectly. You apply for the job and get hired, thanks to your connection with that person.

Another example could be that you are an entrepreneur who wants to build a successful business. You attend industry conferences and events, network with other entrepreneurs and business leaders, and build a strong online presence. As a result, you build a large network of contacts who can offer advice, mentorship, and support. When you face challenges in your business, you can turn to your network for guidance and support, which can help you overcome those challenges and continue to grow your business.

Building a large professional network is essential for long-term career success. It can provide you with opportunities, knowledge sharing, industry trends, and support, which can help you achieve your career goals over a long period of time.

Building a large professional network at the early stage of your career is crucial to set the foundation for long-term success. Here are a few tips on how to build your network:

Attend networking events: Attend events and conferences related to your industry or area of interest. This is a great way to meet new people and expand your network. Look for events where you can interact with others, such as roundtable discussions or workshops.

Join professional organizations: Joining professional organizations related to your field can help you connect with like-minded individuals and expand your network. These organizations often host events and provide opportunities for networking and professional development.

Connect with colleagues and mentors: Take the time to connect with your colleagues and mentors at work. Building relationships with those in your industry can help you stay informed of trends and opportunities in your field.

Use social media: Social media platforms such as LinkedIn and Twitter can be great tools for building your network. Follow industry leaders and engage with their content by commenting and sharing. This can help you establish connections and grow your network.

Volunteer or participate in community activities: Volunteering for organizations or participating in community activities related to your industry can help you meet new people and expand your network while also giving back to your community.

When considering the types of people to make connections with, it's important to look for individuals who share your interests or have experience and knowledge in your field. Consider connecting with colleagues, mentors, and individuals at networking events who work in your industry or have similar goals and interests. Don't limit yourself to only connecting with people who are in the same role or industry as you - building a diverse network can bring new perspectives and opportunities. Remember, building a professional network takes time and effort, so be patient and persistent in your efforts.

<u>Here are some of the top professional networking websites in the world:</u>

LinkedIn: LinkedIn is the largest professional networking website in the world, with over 700 million members. It allows individuals to create a professional profile, connect with others in their industry, join groups, and search for job opportunities.

Meetup: Meetup is a platform that allows individuals to connect with others in their local community who share similar interests. It can be a great way to network with like-minded individuals and attend events related to your industry.

XING: XING is a professional networking website that is popular in Europe. It allows individuals to create a professional profile, connect with others in their industry, join groups, and search for job opportunities.

Opportunity: Opportunity is a professional networking website that is focused on connecting individuals from underrepresented communities with job opportunities. It provides a platform for individuals to create a professional profile, connect with others in their industry, and search for job opportunities.

AngelList: AngelList is a professional networking website that is focused on connecting individuals with job opportunities in the startup industry. It allows individuals to create a professional profile, connect with others in the startup community, and search for job opportunities.

These professional networking websites can be a valuable resource for individuals looking to expand their professional network, connect with others in their industry, and search for job opportunities. It's important to choose the websites that are most relevant to your industry and career goals and actively engage with others on the platform to maximize the benefits.

Some tips on making LinkedIn profile:

To make an impressive LinkedIn profile that attracts employers on a regular basis, here are some tips:

Complete your profile: Ensure that your profile is complete and up-to-date. Add a professional profile picture, a catchy headline, a summary that highlights your skills and experience, and a list of your work experience and education.

Optimize your profile for keywords: Use relevant keywords in your headline, summary, and work experience to optimize your profile for search engines. This will help employers find your profile when searching for candidates with specific skills or experience.

Showcase your achievements: Use your work experience section to showcase your achievements and quantify your accomplishments with data and statistics. This will help employers see the impact you have made in your previous roles and what you can bring to their organization.

Build your network: Connect with others in your industry and engage with their content to build your network. This can help you stay informed of industry trends and potentially lead to job opportunities.

Get endorsements and recommendations: Ask former colleagues or supervisors to endorse your skills and provide recommendations on your profile. This can provide social proof of your abilities and help you stand out to potential employers.

Share relevant content: Share articles, industry news, or your own content that is relevant to your industry or area of expertise. This can demonstrate your knowledge and thought leadership in your field.

Keep your profile up-to-date: Regularly update your profile with new work experience, skills, or education. This can help your profile appear at the top of search results and show employers that you are actively engaged in your career.

By following these tips, you can create an impressive LinkedIn profile that attracts employers on a regular basis and helps you advance in your career.

Your future career plans

A proper career plan is essential for anyone who wants to achieve their professional goals and advance in their career. It provides a roadmap for where you want to go and how you plan to get there, and helps you make informed decisions about your education, skills development, and job opportunities. In this chapter, we will explore the importance of having a proper career plan and how it can help you achieve success in your career.

First and foremost, having a career plan can help you set clear and achievable goals. By defining your long-term career aspirations and breaking them down into smaller, achievable milestones, you can create a clear path for yourself and stay focused on your objectives. This can help you avoid feeling aimless or uncertain about your career path, and help you make strategic decisions that move you closer to your goals.

For example, if your long-term career goal is to become a manager in your field, you can break this down into smaller, achievable milestones, such as completing a management course, gaining experience in team leadership, and taking on additional responsibilities at work. By setting these goals, you have a clear idea of what you need to do to achieve your long-term career aspirations, and can stay motivated and focused on your objectives.

A career plan can also help you identify your strengths and weaknesses, and create a plan to address any skill gaps or areas for improvement. By assessing your skills and knowledge against the requirements of your desired career path, you can identify areas where you need to improve and develop a plan to address these gaps. This can help you stay competitive in your industry and position yourself for career advancement.

For example, if you are interested in a career in marketing, but lack experience in digital marketing, you can identify this as a gap in your skillset and take steps to address it. This could involve taking an online course in digital marketing, volunteering for digital marketing projects at work, or seeking mentorship from someone with expertise in this area. By addressing your skill gaps, you can increase your value as a professional and position yourself for career growth.

Furthermore, a career plan can help you make informed decisions about your education and training. By identifying the skills and knowledge required for your desired career path, you can choose education and training programs that are aligned with your career goals. This can help you gain the skills and knowledge you need to succeed in your industry and make informed decisions about your career path.

For example, if your long-term career goal is to become a software engineer, you can identify the skills and knowledge required for this role and choose an education program that provides you with the necessary training. This could involve pursuing a degree in computer science or attending a coding bootcamp. By choosing an education program that aligns with your career goals, you can gain the skills and knowledge you need to succeed in your industry.

In addition to these benefits, having a career plan can also help you stay focused and motivated in your career. By setting clear goals and objectives, you have a clear idea of what you want to achieve and can stay motivated and focused on your career path. This can help you overcome obstacles and setbacks, and stay committed to your professional development.

For example, if you experience a setback in your career, such as a job loss or rejection from a job opportunity, having a career plan can help you stay focused on your long-term career goals and take strategic steps to get back on track. By having a clear idea of what you want to achieve and how you plan to get there, you can overcome obstacles and stay committed to your career path.

Deciding on your future career plan can be a challenging and sometimes overwhelming process. Here are some steps you can take to help you make informed decisions and create a plan for your career:

Self-assessment: Start by reflecting on your interests, values, strengths, and weaknesses. Consider what you enjoy doing, what motivates you, and what skills and abilities you have. This will help you identify potential career paths that align with your strengths and interests.

Research: Once you have a list of potential career paths, research them to gain a better understanding of the roles, job responsibilities, required education and qualifications, salary ranges, and job outlook. This information can help you make informed decisions and narrow down your list of potential career paths.

Gain experience: If possible, try to gain practical experience in the fields that interest you. This can help you confirm your interest in a particular career and gain valuable skills and knowledge. Consider internships, volunteer work, part-time jobs, or shadowing professionals in the field.

Set goals: Once you have identified potential career paths, set specific, measurable, achievable, relevant, and time-bound (SMART) goals for yourself. These goals can help you stay focused and motivated as you work towards your career objectives.

Develop a plan: Use the information you have gathered to create a career plan that outlines your short-term and long-term goals, the steps you need to take to achieve them, and any potential obstacles or challenges you may face. This plan can serve as a roadmap to help guide your career decisions and keep you on track towards your objectives.

Your career plan may evolve over time as your interests and goals change, so it is important to revisit and adjust it as needed. By taking the time to assess your interests, research potential career paths, gain experience, set goals, and develop a plan, you can make informed decisions and create a roadmap for a successful and fulfilling career.

Inflation

Inflation is a concept that refers to the general increase in the prices of goods and services in an economy over time. It is usually measured using an inflation rate, which represents the percentage increase in the overall price level of a basket of goods and services over a specified period.

<u>The formula for calculating inflation rate is:</u>

Inflation Rate = (Current CPI - Previous CPI) / Previous CPI * 100

Where CPI stands for Consumer Price Index, which is a measure of the average change in prices of a basket of goods and services consumed by households.

Let's take an example to illustrate the concept of inflation. Suppose the CPI for the current year is 150, and the CPI for the previous year was 140. Using the above formula, we can calculate the inflation rate as:

Inflation Rate = (150 - 140) / 140 * 100 = 7.14%

This means that the overall price level of goods and services in the economy has increased by 7.14% over the past year.

Inflation can have various impacts on the economy, such as reducing the purchasing power of consumers, increasing the cost of borrowing for businesses and individuals, and affecting the competitiveness of exports. Central banks and governments often use monetary and fiscal policies to manage inflation and maintain price stability in the economy.

Inflation can be caused by various factors, such as supply and demand imbalances, changes in production costs, changes in exchange rates, and changes in monetary policy. Understanding inflation and its causes is essential for policymakers, businesses, and individuals to make informed decisions and manage risks in an economy.

Is inflation rate same for every one of us?

No, the inflation rate is not the same for everyone. Inflation affects individuals differently depending on their spending patterns and the goods and services they consume.

The Consumer Price Index (CPI) is used to measure inflation, and it is based on a basket of goods and services that represent the average expenditures of households in an economy. However, individual households may have different spending patterns and consume different goods and services, which can result in different rates of inflation for different households.

For example, if an individual spends a larger proportion of their income on healthcare, and the cost of healthcare services increases faster than the overall inflation rate, then they may experience a higher inflation rate than the average. On the other hand, if an individual spends a larger proportion of their income on goods that experience a slower rate of inflation, such as technology, then they may experience a lower inflation rate than the average.

In addition, inflation can also vary across regions and countries due to differences in the availability of goods and services, production costs, exchange rates, and other factors.

Therefore, it is important to consider the individual circumstances and spending patterns when assessing the impact of inflation on different households and individuals.

There are several ways that individuals can protect their wealth from the effects of inflation. Some of these strategies include investing in assets that tend to appreciate in value over time, such as stocks, real estate, and commodities, and investing in assets that generate income that can keep up with inflation, such as dividend-paying stocks and rental properties.

Here are some calculations to illustrate the impact of inflation and how various strategies can help protect wealth:

Impact of inflation on cash savings:

Suppose an individual has 100,000 in cash savings and the inflation rate is 3%. If the individual keeps the money in a savings account with an interest rate of 0.5%, after one year, the real value of their savings will have decreased by:

Inflation rate = 3% Interest rate = 0.5% Real interest rate = -2.5%

Real value of savings after one year = 100,000 * (1 - 2.5%) = 97,500

To protect their wealth from inflation, the individual may consider investing in assets that have the potential to generate higher returns than the inflation rate.

Investing in stocks:

Suppose the individual decides to invest 100,000 in a stock portfolio that generates an average annual return of 7%, which is higher than the inflation rate. After one year, the value of the portfolio would be:

Initial investment = 100,000 Average annual return = 7% Value of portfolio after one year = 100,000 * (1 + 7%) = 107,000

In this scenario, the individual has not only protected their wealth from inflation but has also generated a positive return on their investment.

Investing in real estate:

Suppose the individual decides to invest 100,000 in a rental property that generates an annual net rental income of 10,000 and an average annual price appreciation of 3%, which is equal to the inflation rate. After one year, the value of the property would be:

Initial investment = 100,000 Net rental income = 10,000 Price appreciation = 3% Value of property after one year = 100,000 + 10,000 + (100,000 * 3%) = 113,000

In this scenario, the individual has protected their wealth from inflation through both the rental income and the appreciation in the value of the property.

Investing in commodities:

Suppose the individual decides to invest 100,000 in a commodity such as gold that tends to appreciate in value during periods of inflation. If the price of gold increases by 5% over the course of one year, the value of their investment would be:

Initial investment = 100,000 Price appreciation = 5% Value of investment after one year = 100,000 * (1 + 5%) = 105,000

In this scenario, the individual has protected their wealth from inflation through the appreciation in the value of the commodity.

In summary, protecting wealth from inflation requires investing in assets that can generate returns that keep up with or exceed the inflation rate. By diversifying investments across a range of asset classes, individuals can mitigate the impact of inflation on their wealth and achieve long-term financial stability.

There are several misconceptions about inflation that can lead to misunderstandings about its causes and effects. Here are a few common misconceptions about inflation:

Inflation is always bad:

One common misconception about inflation is that it is always bad for the economy. While high inflation rates can be problematic, low levels of inflation are actually desirable because they indicate a healthy and growing economy. Inflation can be a sign of increased demand for goods and services, which can lead to higher wages and increased job opportunities.

Inflation is caused by rising prices:

Another common misconception is that inflation is caused by rising prices. While rising prices are a symptom of inflation, the root cause of inflation is actually an increase in the money supply. When there is more money in circulation, each individual unit of currency becomes less valuable, which leads to higher prices.

Inflation affects everyone equally:

Many people assume that inflation affects everyone in the same way, but in reality, inflation can have a disproportionate impact on different groups of people. For example, those on fixed incomes, such as retirees or people with disabilities, may have a harder time keeping up with rising prices, while those with investments in assets that appreciate in value during periods of inflation may actually benefit.

Inflation is always caused by government policies:

While government policies can contribute to inflation, they are not always the primary cause. Inflation can also be caused by external factors such as changes in global commodity prices, natural disasters, or shifts in international trade patterns.

Inflation is always a result of excessive money printing:

While increasing the money supply can lead to inflation, it is not the only way that inflation can occur. Inflation can also be caused by changes in demand for goods and services, changes in the supply of goods and services, or changes in the velocity of money (how quickly money changes hands in the economy).

Understanding the true causes and effects of inflation is crucial for making informed decisions about personal finance and economic policy. By dispelling these common misconceptions, individuals can develop a more accurate understanding of how inflation works and how to protect themselves from its negative effects.

Inflation, defined as the rate at which the general level of prices for goods and services is rising, is often viewed as a negative economic phenomenon that can have detrimental effects on individuals and the economy as a whole. However, there are also positive sides to inflation that are often overlooked. In this chapter, we will discuss some of the positive aspects of inflation.

One of the primary positive effects of inflation is that it can stimulate economic growth. When prices are rising, consumers are often motivated to purchase goods and services sooner rather than later, as they expect prices to continue to rise. This increased demand can lead to an increase in production, which in turn can create jobs and contribute to economic growth. Additionally, higher prices can incentivize businesses to invest in new technology and research and development, which can improve efficiency and productivity.

Another positive aspect of inflation is that it can help to reduce debt burdens. When inflation occurs, the value of money decreases over time. This means that the amount of debt owed in real terms is reduced. For example, if someone borrowed 10,000 at a 5% interest rate and inflation increased by 3%, the value of the debt would be reduced to 9,700 in real terms. This can help to ease the burden of debt for individuals and businesses.

Inflation can also help to reduce unemployment rates. When prices are rising, businesses may be more likely to invest in new equipment and hire additional workers in order to keep up with demand. This can lead to a decrease in unemployment rates, which can have positive effects on the overall economy.

Furthermore, inflation can help to stimulate investment in assets such as stocks, real estate, and commodities. As prices rise, the value of these assets may also increase, providing an opportunity for investors to make a profit. This can help to promote economic growth and encourage investment in new projects and businesses.

Lastly, inflation can encourage individuals and businesses to save money. When prices are rising, individuals may be more likely to save money in order to avoid the negative effects of inflation. This can lead to increased savings rates, which can provide a source of capital for businesses and help to promote economic growth.

While inflation is often viewed as a negative economic phenomenon, there are also positive aspects to consider. Inflation can stimulate economic growth, reduce debt burdens, reduce unemployment rates, stimulate investment, and encourage savings. It is important to strike a balance between controlling inflation and promoting economic growth in order to achieve a healthy and sustainable economy.

Generating passive income

Passive income refers to any income earned without active involvement or effort on the part of the recipient. In other words, passive income is generated through investments, real estate, and other sources that require minimal ongoing effort once established. In this chapter, we will discuss what passive income is, the benefits of having passive income, and some strategies for generating passive income.

Passive income can take many forms, including rental income from real estate, dividends from stocks, royalties from intellectual property, and income from affiliate marketing or online businesses. The common thread among all of these sources is that they require little to no active involvement once established, and can continue to generate income over time.

There are several benefits to having passive income in life. First, passive income can provide financial security and stability. With a steady stream of income coming in from various sources, individuals can feel more secure in their financial future and less reliant on a single source of income. This can help to reduce financial stress and provide greater peace of mind.

Second, passive income can provide greater flexibility and freedom in terms of career and lifestyle choices. With income coming in from various sources, individuals may have more freedom to pursue their passions and interests, rather than being tied to a single job or career path. Additionally, passive income can provide greater flexibility in terms of work schedule and location, allowing individuals to work from anywhere and at any time.

Third, passive income can help to build wealth over time. By investing in assets that generate passive income, individuals can build wealth and accumulate assets that can provide long-term financial security. This can help to create a legacy for future generations and provide a source of financial stability for years to come.

There are many strategies for generating passive income. One of the most popular strategies is real estate investing. By purchasing rental properties, individuals can generate passive income through monthly rental payments. Additionally, real estate can appreciate in value over time, providing an opportunity for long-term wealth building.

Another strategy for generating passive income is dividend investing. By investing in dividend-paying stocks, individuals can earn a steady stream of income through regular dividend payments. Additionally, dividend stocks can appreciate in value over time, providing an opportunity for long-term wealth building.

Affiliate marketing and online businesses can also be a source of passive income. By creating a website or blog and promoting affiliate products, individuals can earn a commission on sales made through their website. Additionally, online businesses such as e-commerce stores can generate passive income through ongoing sales.

In conclusion, passive income is a valuable source of income that can provide financial security, flexibility, and long-term wealth building opportunities. By investing in assets that generate passive income, individuals can reduce financial stress, pursue their passions, and build a legacy for future generations. There are many strategies for generating passive income, including real estate investing, dividend investing, and online businesses. With careful planning and strategic investments, anyone can create a steady stream of passive income that can provide financial security for years to come.

Rich people often focus on passive income because it provides a number of benefits that active income does not. First, passive income can provide greater financial security and stability, as it is not reliant on a single source of income. This can help to reduce financial stress and provide greater peace of mind.

Second, passive income can provide greater flexibility and freedom in terms of lifestyle and career choices. With income coming in from various sources, rich individuals may have more freedom to pursue their passions and interests, rather than being tied to a single job or career path. Additionally, passive income can provide greater flexibility in terms of work schedule and location, allowing individuals to work from anywhere and at any time.

Third, passive income can help to build wealth over time. By investing in assets that generate passive income, rich individuals can build wealth and accumulate assets that can provide long-term financial security. This can help to create a legacy for future generations and provide a source of financial stability for years to come.

Furthermore, rich people often have a greater understanding of the power of compounding. By reinvesting passive income back into their investments, they can generate even more passive income over time, leading to exponential growth in their wealth. This can be particularly powerful when combined with long-term investments that appreciate in value over time, such as real estate or dividend-paying stocks.

The answer to which income is better - active or passive - depends on the individual's financial goals and circumstances. Both types of income have their advantages and disadvantages.

Active income is earned through work or services provided by an individual. This could be a salary, wages, commissions, or profits from a business. The advantage of active income is that it is usually predictable, consistent, and immediate. For example, if someone earns a salary of 50,000 per year, they know exactly how much income they will receive each month. However, the disadvantage of active income is that it is usually limited by time and effort. If the individual stops working or providing services, the income stops as well.

Passive income, on the other hand, is earned without active involvement. This could be through investments, rental properties, or royalties from creative works. The advantage of passive income is that it can be earned without the need for constant effort, allowing individuals to have more free time and pursue other interests. Additionally, passive income can be scalable, meaning it can grow over time without the need for additional effort. However, the disadvantage of passive income is that it may take time and effort to set up, and it may not be as consistent or predictable as active income.

To compare the two types of income, let's consider an example:

Assume that two individuals, Ram and Sam, each have a net worth of 500,000. Ram earns an active income of 100,000 per year as a software engineer, while Sam earns a passive income of 5% per year from her investment portfolio.

After 10 years, assuming they do not make any additional investments or changes to their income, their net worth will be:

Ram's net worth = 1,000,000 (active income only) Sam's net worth = 814,447.09 (passive income only)

As we can see from this example, both types of income can lead to significant wealth accumulation over time. However, passive income has the potential to grow exponentially over time, while active income is limited by the individual's time and effort.

Whether active income or passive income is better depends on an individual's financial goals, risk tolerance, and circumstances. Active income can provide a steady and predictable source of income, while passive income can provide more freedom and potential for exponential growth. It may be beneficial to have a combination of both types of income to achieve financial security and flexibility.

Your negotiation skills

Negotiation skills refer to the ability to communicate effectively and reach a mutual agreement with another party, often involving the exchange of goods, services, or ideas. Developing strong negotiation skills can be essential in both personal and professional contexts, as it can help individuals achieve their goals, resolve conflicts, and build stronger relationships.

Here are some ways to develop strong negotiation skills:

Understand the goals and needs of both parties: It is essential to understand the goals and needs of both parties involved in the negotiation. This can help you find common ground and identify potential solutions that meet the needs of both parties.

Prepare and practice: Before entering a negotiation, it can be helpful to prepare by researching the topic and practicing your negotiation skills. This can help you feel more confident and prepared during the negotiation.

Active listening: Active listening is a crucial component of successful negotiation. It involves paying attention to the other party's perspective, asking clarifying questions, and demonstrating empathy and understanding.

Communication skills: Effective communication skills, including clear and concise verbal and nonverbal communication, can be essential in successful negotiation.

Flexibility and creativity: Sometimes, negotiations may require creative solutions or flexibility to reach a mutually beneficial agreement. Being open to different ideas and approaches can help you find creative solutions that work for both parties.

Conflict resolution: Negotiation often involves conflict, and the ability to manage and resolve conflict can be critical in achieving a successful negotiation outcome.

Emotional intelligence: Emotional intelligence involves understanding and managing your own emotions and the emotions of others. It can help you build rapport and establish a positive relationship with the other party, leading to a more successful negotiation outcome.

Developing strong negotiation skills can take time and practice, but it can be a valuable skill to have in both personal and professional contexts. By understanding the goals and needs of both parties, preparing and practicing, active listening, effective communication, flexibility and creativity, conflict resolution, and emotional intelligence, you can develop strong negotiation skills and achieve your desired outcomes.

<u>Some of the best negotiator in the world:</u>

It is difficult to determine who the best negotiator in the world is, as negotiation skills are subjective and can vary depending on the context and situation. However, there are some individuals who are widely recognized for their exceptional negotiation skills and have achieved great success in their respective fields.

One individual who is often cited as an exceptional negotiator is former U.S. Secretary of State, Henry Kissinger. He is credited with negotiating the end of the Vietnam War, as well as the opening of diplomatic relations between the U.S. and China. His negotiation skills were characterized by his ability to understand the goals and needs of both parties, as well as his flexibility and creativity in finding solutions that met the needs of both sides.

Another individual who is often cited as a great negotiator is Nelson Mandela. As a key figure in ending apartheid in South Africa, Mandela was known for his ability to build relationships and establish trust with those he was negotiating with. He also demonstrated empathy and understanding, which helped him bridge divides and find common ground.

In the business world, Elon Musk is often cited as a great negotiator. His negotiation skills have helped him secure deals with major car manufacturers and suppliers, as well as secure government contracts for SpaceX. Musk is known for his ability to communicate his vision and goals clearly, as well as his willingness to take risks and think creatively in negotiations.

Ultimately, the best negotiator in the world will depend on the context and situation. However, individuals like Kissinger, Mandela, and Musk demonstrate the importance of understanding the goals and needs of both parties, building relationships and trust, demonstrating empathy and understanding, and thinking creatively to find mutually beneficial solutions.

Pure Public Goods

In economics, a pure public good is a type of good that is non-excludable and non-rivalrous. This means that once the good is provided, it is available to everyone and no one can be prevented from using it. Additionally, one person's consumption of the good does not diminish the amount available for others to use.

A classic example of a pure public good is national defence. Once a country has a defence system in place, everyone within that country benefits from the protection it provides, regardless of whether they paid for it or not. It is impossible to exclude anyone from the benefits of national defence, and the fact that one person is benefiting from it does not diminish the benefits that others receive.

Another example of a pure public good is clean air. Once the air is clean, everyone can breathe it without any reduction in the quality of the air available for others to breathe. It is difficult, if not impossible, to exclude someone from the benefits of clean air, and the fact that one person is breathing the air does not reduce the amount of clean air available for others to breathe.

Pure public goods are generally considered to be underprovided by the private sector, as there is no way for companies to profit from providing them. Therefore, governments often step in to provide pure public goods, using taxes to finance their provision.

Here are some other examples of pure public goods in India:

Law and order: The government provides police services, the court system, and other measures to maintain law and order, which benefits everyone in the country.

Basic infrastructure: Roads, bridges, and public transportation systems are examples of pure public goods that are provided by the government and used by all citizens.

Public health: The government provides health services, sanitation systems, and other measures to improve public health, which benefits everyone in the country.

Public education: The government provides education services to all citizens, regardless of their ability to pay, which benefits the entire society by producing an educated and productive workforce.

Public parks and recreational facilities: The government provides parks, playgrounds, and other recreational facilities that are open to everyone, regardless of their ability to pay.

These are just a few examples of the pure public goods provided by the Indian government.

Pure public goods in India are primarily controlled and provided by the government, which is responsible for their provision, financing, and management. In India, the provision of pure public goods is often the responsibility of different levels of government, including the central government, state governments, and local governments.

For example, national defence is primarily the responsibility of the central government, while basic infrastructure such as roads and bridges may be the responsibility of state or local governments. Similarly, public health services and public education may be provided by state or local governments, while clean air and water are the responsibility of both central and state governments.

The government uses taxes and other sources of revenue to finance the provision of pure public goods, and it has the authority to regulate and manage their use. The government also has the responsibility to ensure that these goods are provided in a way that is equitable and accessible to all citizens, regardless of their socioeconomic status. Overall, the government plays a crucial role in controlling and providing pure public goods in India.

Having pure public goods in any economy is important for several reasons:

Non-exclusion: Pure public goods are goods that cannot be excluded from anyone, which means that everyone has access to them. This ensures that all citizens can benefit from the goods without being left out or discriminated against based on their income, social status, or any other factor.

Non-rivalrous: Pure public goods are also non-rivalrous, meaning that the use of the goods by one person does not reduce the availability or quality of the goods for others. This means that more people can benefit from these goods without causing depletion or deterioration of their quality.

Positive externalities: Pure public goods often have positive externalities, which means that the benefits of the goods spill over to other areas of the economy. For example, investments in public health can lead to a healthier population, which in turn can lead to a more productive workforce and a stronger economy.

Economic growth: Pure public goods can contribute to economic growth by providing the necessary infrastructure, education, and other public services that are needed for a strong and sustainable economy.

Social welfare: Pure public goods can contribute to social welfare by providing essential services that are necessary for a decent standard of living, such as access to clean water, sanitation, and education.

Having pure public goods in any economy is important for promoting equity, economic growth, and social welfare. The provision of these goods is often the responsibility of the government, which uses taxes and other sources of revenue to finance their provision and ensure that they are accessible to all citizens.

Forged Currency & its effects on the economy

Forged currency, also known as counterfeit currency, refers to currency that is illegally produced and circulated in an economy. It is a significant problem for economies around the world, as it can have severe economic, social, and political consequences. Counterfeit currency is usually produced with the intention of making a profit, often through illegal means, such as drug trafficking, arms dealing, and other criminal activities.

How is Counterfeit Currency Produced?

Counterfeit currency is produced using a variety of methods, depending on the type of currency being counterfeited. For paper currency, counterfeiters may use printers, scanners, and other digital devices to create a high-quality copy of the currency. They may use special paper, ink, and other materials to make the counterfeit currency look as close to the real thing as possible. Counterfeiters may also use old printing presses, lithographs, and other traditional printing methods to produce counterfeit currency.

For coins, counterfeiters may use metal alloys and other materials to create a counterfeit coin that looks and feels like a genuine coin. They may use advanced techniques, such as laser engraving, to create intricate designs and patterns on the coin to make it look more genuine.

For digital currency, counterfeiters may use hacking techniques to steal digital currency from legitimate sources, such as digital wallets or online exchanges. They may also use malware or other malicious software to infect computer systems and steal digital currency.

Effects of Counterfeit Currency on the Economy:

Counterfeit currency can have significant effects on the economy, both in the short term and in the long term. Some of the effects of counterfeit currency on the economy include:

Reduction in Confidence: Counterfeit currency can reduce confidence in the economy and in the currency itself. When people lose confidence in the currency, they may be less likely to use it, which can lead to a reduction in economic activity.

Inflation: Counterfeit currency can lead to inflation, as the increased supply of money can lead to an increase in prices. This can make it more difficult for people to afford goods and services, and can lead to a decrease in economic growth.

Losses to Businesses: Counterfeit currency can lead to losses for businesses, particularly those that handle a lot of cash, such as retail stores and restaurants. When counterfeit currency is used to purchase goods or services, businesses lose out on the revenue that they would have received if genuine currency had been used.

Cost to Government: Governments often bear the cost of counterfeiting investigations and prosecution, as well as the cost of replacing counterfeit currency with genuine currency. This can be a significant burden on government resources.

Damage to Reputation: Counterfeit currency can damage the reputation of a country or currency, particularly if the counterfeit currency is of high quality and difficult to detect. This can have a negative impact on trade and investment, and can harm the overall economic growth of a country.

Increased Crime: Counterfeit currency is often associated with organized crime, and its production and distribution may be linked to other illegal activities, such as drug trafficking and arms dealing. The presence of counterfeit currency in an economy can led to an increase in crime, which can have a negative impact on the overall safety and security of a country.

Preventing counterfeit currency is a critical challenge for governments and central banks around the world. There are several steps that can be taken to prevent counterfeit currency:

Education: Educating the public about how to detect counterfeit currency can be an effective way to reduce its circulation. Governments can launch public awareness campaigns to educate people about the security features of genuine currency, such as watermarks, microprinting, and holograms. This can help people identify counterfeit currency and avoid accepting it.

Improved Security Features: Currency can be designed with improved security features that make it more difficult to counterfeit. For example, some currencies now use special paper that is difficult to reproduce, while others use holograms, colour-shifting inks, and other features that are hard to replicate. Currency designers can continue to explore new technologies and materials that make currency more secure.

Law Enforcement: Governments can increase their efforts to investigate and prosecute counterfeiters. This can include working with international law enforcement agencies to track down counterfeiters who operate across borders. Governments can also impose stiff penalties on those caught producing or distributing counterfeit currency to deter others from engaging in this illegal activity.

Collaboration with Financial Institutions: Financial institutions, such as banks and money exchanges, can play a critical role in preventing the circulation of counterfeit currency. They can use specialized machines to detect counterfeit currency and provide training to their employees on how to recognize counterfeit currency. Governments can work with financial institutions to establish reporting mechanisms for suspected counterfeit currency, which can help to identify and track counterfeiters.

Public-Private Partnerships: Public-private partnerships can bring together government agencies, financial institutions, and other stakeholders to share information and collaborate on anti-counterfeit measures. For example, governments can work with technology companies to develop new security features for currency or with retailers to improve their ability to detect counterfeit currency.

Continuous Innovation: The fight against counterfeit currency is an ongoing battle, and counterfeiters are continually looking for new ways to produce high-quality counterfeit currency. To stay ahead of counterfeiters, currency designers and law enforcement agencies need to continuously innovate and explore new technologies and strategies to prevent the production and circulation of counterfeit currency.

Rudraksha

Rudraksha is a seed that comes from the Elaeocarpus ganitrus tree, which is primarily found in Nepal, Indonesia, and India. The seed has been used for thousands of years in Hinduism and Buddhism as a spiritual tool for meditation and healing. Rudraksha beads are considered sacred and are believed to offer numerous spiritual and health benefits. There are various types of Rudraksha beads available, which are categorized based on the number of faces or mukhis they have.

Here are the different types of Rudraksha beads and their corresponding benefits:

Ek Mukhi Rudraksha: The Ek Mukhi Rudraksha is a single-faced bead, which is considered the most powerful and rarest of all Rudraksha beads. It is believed to bring wealth, prosperity, and success to the wearer. It is also said to help in attaining liberation and spiritual enlightenment.

Do Mukhi Rudraksha: The Do Mukhi Rudraksha is a two-faced bead, which represents the divine couple Shiva and Parvati. It is believed to help in balancing the mind, improving relationships, and promoting harmony and unity.

Teen Mukhi Rudraksha: The Teen Mukhi Rudraksha is a three-faced bead, which represents the three deities Brahma, Vishnu, and Mahesh. It is believed to provide good health, wealth, and wisdom to the wearer.

Chatur Mukhi Rudraksha: The Chatur Mukhi Rudraksha is a four-faced bead, which represents the four-headed Lord Brahma. It is believed to help in improving intelligence, memory, and creativity.

Panch Mukhi Rudraksha: The Panch Mukhi Rudraksha is a five-faced bead, which represents the five elements of nature - earth, water, fire, air, and space. It is believed to help in promoting peace, harmony, and prosperity.

Shat Mukhi Rudraksha: The Shat Mukhi Rudraksha is a six-faced bead, which represents the six virtues of human life - love, peace, health, prosperity, wisdom, and contentment. It is believed to help in balancing emotions, promoting mental clarity, and improving relationships.

Sapta Mukhi Rudraksha: The Sapta Mukhi Rudraksha is a seven-faced bead, which represents the seven divine mothers - Brahmi, Maheshwari, Kaumari, Vaishnavi, Varahi, Indrani, and Chamunda. It is believed to provide good health, wealth, and success to the wearer.

Asht Mukhi Rudraksha: The Asht Mukhi Rudraksha is an eight-faced bead, which represents the eight forms of Lord Ganesha. It is believed to help in removing obstacles, promoting success, and providing mental peace.

Nau Mukhi Rudraksha: The Nau Mukhi Rudraksha is a nine-faced bead, which represents the nine forms of the goddess Durga. It is believed to help in promoting mental and physical strength, courage, and confidence.

Dasha Mukhi Rudraksha: The Dasha Mukhi Rudraksha is a ten-faced bead, which represents the ten directions - north, south, east, west, northeast, northwest, southeast, southwest, upward, and downward. It is believed to help in promoting good health, wealth, and prosperity.

Rudraksha beads contain several bioactive compounds, including alkaloids, flavonoids, tannins, and steroids, which have been found to exhibit antioxidant, anti-inflammatory, and antimicrobial properties. One of the most studied bioactive compounds in Rudraksha is a group of alkaloids known as indole alkaloids, which are also found in other plants such as coffee, tea, and chocolate.

Research has shown that indole alkaloids in Rudraksha can inhibit the growth of cancer cells and reduce oxidative stress in the body. They have also been found to have neuroprotective effects and can help in reducing inflammation in the brain, which may be beneficial in the treatment of neurological disorders such as Alzheimer's and Parkinson's disease.

In terms of the chemical structure of Rudraksha, the seed contains high levels of carbon, hydrogen, oxygen, and nitrogen, along with trace amounts of other elements such as calcium, iron, and magnesium. The outer surface of the seed contains a hard, thick layer of cellulose, which protects the inner seed from damage.

Rudraksha is a plant seed and therefore has a scientific basis in terms of its chemical composition and biological properties. However, in Indian culture, Rudraksha is also considered to have spiritual and religious significance. It is believed to have healing and protective properties and is often worn as a mala (prayer beads) by people following Hinduism, Buddhism, and other spiritual practices. The spiritual significance of Rudraksha is not based on scientific evidence but rather on traditional beliefs and cultural practices. Therefore, it can be viewed as both a scientific and a spiritual thing, depending on one's perspective and beliefs.

Snake venom

Despite its potentially deadly effects, snake venom has been used for centuries to produce a wide range of medical treatments. This is because snake venom contains a complex mixture of biologically active compounds that have a range of therapeutic properties.

One of the most well-known uses of snake venom is in the production of antivenom. Antivenom is a medication that is administered to individuals who have been bitten by a venomous snake. It works by neutralizing the effects of the venom in the body, and preventing further damage to tissues and organs. To produce antivenom, scientists extract small amounts of venom from snakes, and then inject it into horses or other animals. These animals produce antibodies that can bind to and neutralize the venom. The antibodies are then purified and used to produce antivenom for human use.

In addition to antivenom, snake venom has also been used to develop a range of other medications. For example, some compounds found in snake venom have been shown to have anticoagulant properties, meaning they can prevent blood from clotting. These compounds have been used to develop medications that can help prevent blood clots, such as those that can lead to heart attacks and strokes.

Other compounds found in snake venom have been shown to have analgesic properties, meaning they can reduce pain. These compounds have been used to develop pain-relieving medications that are used to treat a variety of conditions, from headaches to chronic pain.

Finally, some compounds found in snake venom have been shown to have anti-cancer properties. These compounds can prevent cancer cells from growing and dividing, and can even induce apoptosis, or programmed cell death, in cancer cells. Researchers are currently studying these compounds to develop new cancer treatments.

In conclusion, snake venom contains a complex mixture of biologically active compounds that have a range of therapeutic properties. While it can be dangerous if not properly handled, when used under controlled conditions, it has the potential to lead to the development of new and effective medical treatments.

Why sky is Blue?

The blue colour of the sky is due to a phenomenon called Rayleigh scattering. This is a type of scattering that occurs when light passes through a medium, such as the Earth's atmosphere, and encounters particles that are much smaller than the wavelength of the light.

The Earth's atmosphere contains a variety of particles, including molecules of nitrogen, oxygen, and other gases, as well as tiny particles of dust, water vapor, and other substances. When sunlight enters the atmosphere, it encounters these particles, which cause the light to scatter in different directions.

The amount of scattering that occurs depends on the wavelength of the light. Shorter-wavelength light, such as blue and violet, is scattered much more than longer-wavelength light, such as red and orange. This is because the particles in the atmosphere are much smaller than the wavelength of blue and violet light, which makes them much more effective at scattering this type of light.

As a result of this scattering, blue and violet light is scattered in all directions, filling the sky with a blue hue. This is why the sky appears blue to our eyes during the daytime. At sunset or sunrise, when the sun is lower on the horizon, the light has to pass through more of the Earth's atmosphere, which scatters away even more of the blue and violet light. This makes the sky appear reddish or orange.

In summary, the blue colour of the sky is due to a phenomenon called Rayleigh scattering, which occurs when sunlight passes through the Earth's atmosphere and encounters small particles that scatter shorter-wavelength light, such as blue and violet, more effectively than longer-wavelength light, such as red and orange.

Metaverse

The metaverse is a term used to describe a virtual world that is created by the convergence of virtual reality, augmented reality, and the internet. It is a shared digital space that is accessible to anyone with an internet connection and can be accessed through a variety of devices, such as virtual reality headsets, smartphones, and computers. In the metaverse, users can interact with each other and with digital objects in a way that is similar to the physical world, but with added features and possibilities.

One example of the metaverse in action is the online game Second Life. In Second Life, users create avatars, which are digital representations of themselves, and explore a virtual world that is populated by other users and digital objects. Users can interact with each other, attend events, and even buy and sell virtual goods using a digital currency.

Another example of the metaverse is the game Fortnite, which has become a popular platform for hosting virtual concerts and events. In 2019, Fortnite hosted a concert by the DJ Marshmello, which was attended by more than 10 million players. The concert took place within the game, with players able to interact with the digital environment and with each other during the performance.

The concept of the metaverse has also been explored in literature and film. In Neal Stephenson's novel "Snow Crash," the metaverse is portrayed as a fully immersive digital world that serves as a replacement for the physical world. In the film "The Matrix," the concept of a virtual world that is created and controlled by machines is explored, with humans trapped in the virtual world and unaware of their true physical existence.

Overall, the metaverse is a concept that is still in development, with many different companies and organizations exploring ways to create shared digital spaces that are accessible to anyone with an internet connection. While the potential of the metaverse is still being explored, it has the potential to create new opportunities for social interaction, commerce, and entertainment, as well as new challenges and concerns around privacy, security, and access.

The concept of the metaverse has generated significant excitement and anticipation, as it has the potential to transform the way we interact with each other and with digital content. However, like any new technology, the metaverse also has both positive and negative sides, which must be considered in order to fully understand its potential impact on society. In this response, I will discuss the positive and negative sides of the metaverse in detail.

Positive Sides of Metaverse:

Enhanced Social Interaction: One of the main potential benefits of the metaverse is the ability to enhance social interaction in new and innovative ways. The metaverse can provide a virtual space for people to come together and connect with others who share similar interests, regardless of their physical location. This can provide opportunities for socialization and community building that may not be possible in the physical world.

New Business Opportunities: The metaverse has the potential to create new business opportunities by providing a platform for virtual commerce. This could include the sale of virtual goods, such as digital art and clothing, as well as the creation of new services and experiences that can be delivered through the metaverse. This could create new jobs and revenue streams for businesses and individuals.

Increased Access to Education: The metaverse can also provide opportunities for increased access to education, as it can provide a virtual space for people to learn and collaborate with others. This can be particularly valuable for people who live in remote areas or who have limited access to traditional educational resources.

Improved Accessibility: The metaverse can also provide opportunities for improved accessibility, as it can provide virtual environments that are designed to be more accessible for people with disabilities. For example, virtual environments can be designed to be more navigable for people with mobility impairments or to provide alternative forms of communication for people with hearing or vision impairments.

<u>Negative Sides of Metaverse:</u>

Social Isolation: While the metaverse has the potential to enhance social interaction, it could also lead to increased social isolation, as people may choose to spend more time in virtual environments rather than interacting with others in the physical world. This could lead to a decline in physical social interaction and an increase in mental health issues such as loneliness and depression.

Privacy Concerns: The metaverse raises significant privacy concerns, as users may be required to share personal information in order to participate in virtual environments. This information could be used for targeted advertising or other purposes, which could lead to violations of privacy and other legal issues.

Security Risks: The metaverse also poses significant security risks, as virtual environments could be vulnerable to hacking and other cyber-attacks. This could lead to the loss of personal information or the manipulation of virtual environments, which could have significant consequences for users.

Digital Divide: The metaverse also has the potential to widen the digital divide, as not all individuals or communities may have access to the technology required to participate in virtual environments. This could create new forms of inequality and exclusion.

The metaverse has both positive and negative sides, and it is important to consider both in order to fully understand its potential impact on society. While the metaverse has the potential to enhance social interaction, create new business opportunities, and improve accessibility to education and other resources, it also raises concerns around social isolation, privacy, security, and the digital divide. As the development of the metaverse continues, it will be important to address these concerns in order to create a safe and inclusive digital space for all users.

Your mobile notifications

Mobile notifications are designed to be helpful and informative, providing us with updates on important events, messages from friends and family, and reminders about upcoming appointments. However, there are some darker aspects to mobile notifications that are worth exploring.

One of the key issues with mobile notifications is the way they can be used to manipulate our behaviour. App developers and marketers use a range of techniques to encourage us to engage with their apps, including sending notifications at specific times of day or using push notifications to grab our attention when we are most likely to respond. In some cases, these techniques can be highly effective, leading us to spend more time on our phones and becoming more reliant on particular apps.

Another concern with mobile notifications is the way they can be used to gather data about our behaviour. Many apps use notifications to collect information about how we interact with our phones, including which apps we use, how frequently we check our phones, and what kind of content we consume. This data can be highly valuable to advertisers and other third-party companies, who may use it to build detailed profiles of our behaviour and preferences.

There is also growing evidence to suggest that mobile notifications can have negative impacts on our mental health and well-being. Studies have shown that excessive mobile phone use is associated with a range of negative outcomes, including increased stress and anxiety, poorer sleep quality, and decreased feelings of well-being. Notifications can be a key contributor to these negative outcomes, by encouraging us to spend more time on our phones and creating a constant source of distraction and stress.

Finally, there are concerns around the security of mobile notifications, particularly in relation to data breaches and other forms of cybercrime. Hackers and other malicious actors can use notifications to gain access to our devices or steal sensitive information, putting our privacy and security at risk.

Finally, we can say, while mobile notifications can be helpful and informative, there are some dark secrets to their use that are worth considering. These include their potential to manipulate our behaviour, collect data about our behaviour, and negatively impact our mental health and well-being. It is important for users to be aware of these issues and to take steps to protect their privacy and security when using mobile devices.

Some interesting Economic concepts

Here are some interesting economic concepts:

Opportunity Cost – Opportunity cost is the cost of an alternative that must be forgone to pursue a certain action. It is the value of the next best alternative that is not chosen. In other words, when we make a decision, there is always a cost associated with it - the cost of what we could have chosen but didn't.

For example, let's say you have INR.100 and you are considering whether to spend it on a new video game or save it for a rainy day. If you choose to buy the video game, the opportunity cost is the money you could have saved for a rainy day. Alternatively, if you choose to save the money, the opportunity cost is the enjoyment you could have gained from playing the video game.

Another example is when a student decides to go to college instead of entering the workforce immediately after high school. The opportunity cost is the income that the student could have earned if they had entered the workforce immediately. However, by going to college, the student is investing in their education and increasing their potential for higher earnings in the future.

Opportunity cost is important in decision-making because it helps individuals and businesses make more informed choices. It is a way of weighing the benefits and costs of different options before making a decision. By understanding the opportunity cost of a decision, individuals and businesses can make better use of their resources and avoid making choices that may have negative long-term consequences.

The Tragedy of the Commons - The Tragedy of the Commons is an economic concept that refers to the depletion or overuse of a shared, limited resource due to individuals acting in their own self-interest, rather than in the best interest of the collective group. This can result in a negative outcome for everyone involved.

A common example of the tragedy of the commons is overfishing. In this scenario, a fishing community may have access to a shared body of water with a limited supply of fish. Each fisherman wants to catch as many fish as possible to maximize their own profits, but if everyone overfishes the resource, it can become depleted and may never fully recover. This not only harms the fisherman who may lose their livelihoods, but also affects the broader ecosystem and the local economy that depends on the fishing industry.

Another example of the tragedy of the commons is air pollution. Each factory or individual car owner may not be motivated to reduce their emissions, as it would increase their costs and reduce their profits. However, if everyone continues to pollute the air, it can have severe consequences for the health and well-being of the general public, as well as the environment as a whole.

The tragedy of the commons can occur in any situation where there is a shared, limited resource that can be overused or exploited. It highlights the importance of having regulations and policies in place to manage and conserve these resources for the long-term benefit of society. This can involve things like setting limits on the use of a resource, imposing taxes or fees to discourage overuse, or creating incentives for individuals and businesses to adopt more sustainable practices.

The Paradox of Thrift - The Paradox of Thrift is an economic concept that refers to the idea that if individuals or households increase their savings during an economic downturn, it can actually lead to a further decrease in economic activity and can be harmful to the overall economy. This is because an increase in saving leads to a decrease in consumption, which in turn reduces the overall demand for goods and services, ultimately leading to a reduction in production, employment, and income. In other words, what may be good for an individual or household may not be good for the economy as a whole.

An example of the paradox of thrift can be seen during a recession when individuals and households cut back on their spending and increase their savings to protect themselves from economic uncertainty. While this may make sense for an individual or household, if everyone does the same thing, it can lead to a further decrease in economic activity, resulting in a deeper recession. This is because the decrease in consumption reduces the overall demand for goods and services, which can lead to layoffs and further reductions in income, ultimately perpetuating the economic downturn.

Another example of the paradox of thrift can be seen during a time of low interest rates when individuals and households increase their savings to earn interest income. While this may make sense for an individual or household, if everyone does the same thing, it can lead to a decrease in spending and economic activity, ultimately leading to a decrease in interest rates and a reduction in income for savers.

The paradox of thrift highlights the importance of understanding the interconnectedness of the economy and the potential unintended consequences of individual actions. While saving may be important for individual financial security, it is important to balance this with consumption and spending to support economic growth and stability. This is why government policies often focus on stimulating spending during times of economic downturns through measures like tax cuts, government spending, and low interest rates. By doing so, they hope to boost demand, increase production and employment, and ultimately, support economic recovery.

The Phillips Curve - The Phillips Curve is an economic concept that shows the relationship between unemployment and inflation. The curve suggests that as unemployment decreases, inflation increases and vice versa. The curve is named after the economist A.W. Phillips, who first observed the relationship in the 1950s.

The Phillips Curve can be illustrated through the following example: If the unemployment rate in a country is high, then the demand for labour is low, and this puts downward pressure on wages. As a result, firms can produce goods and services at a lower cost, which can lead to lower prices, or deflation. Conversely, if the unemployment rate is low, then the demand for labour is high, and this puts upward pressure on wages. As a result, firms have to pay more for labour, and this can lead to higher prices, or inflation.

However, the Phillips Curve is not a straightforward concept, and there are many factors that can affect the relationship between unemployment and inflation. For example, the curve may shift depending on changes in expectations, supply shocks, or changes in the structure of the labour market.

In the 1970s, the relationship between unemployment and inflation appeared to break down as inflation remained high even when unemployment was high. This phenomenon was called "stagflation" and led to the development of the concept of the "Non-Accelerating Inflation Rate of Unemployment" (NAIRU). NAIRU represents the level of unemployment at which the inflation rate is stable, and any deviation from this level will lead to changes in the inflation rate.

An example of the Phillips Curve in action can be seen in the United States during the 1960s. The unemployment rate was low, and this led to upward pressure on wages and higher inflation. The government responded by implementing policies to reduce inflation, including tighter monetary policy and wage and price controls. These policies led to higher unemployment, which in turn led to lower inflation.

Another example of the Phillips Curve can be seen in Japan during the 1990s. Japan experienced a period of low economic growth and deflation, which was caused by a combination of factors, including an aging population, a decrease in the workforce, and a reduction in government spending. Despite high levels of unemployment during this period, inflation remained low, which challenged the traditional Phillips Curve relationship.

The Phillips Curve concept remains a useful tool for understanding the relationship between unemployment and inflation, but it is important to consider the many factors that can affect this relationship. In practice, policymakers use the Phillips Curve as a guide when making decisions about monetary and fiscal policy, but they must also consider other factors, such as productivity growth, international trade, and technological change, when making these decisions.

The Laffer Curve - The Laffer Curve is an economic concept that illustrates the relationship between tax rates and tax revenue. The curve suggests that there is a point at which increasing tax rates beyond a certain level will actually decrease tax revenue, as it reduces the incentive for people to work, invest, and engage in economic activity. The curve is named after economist Arthur Laffer, who first proposed the concept in the 1970s.

The Laffer Curve can be illustrated through the following example: If a government imposes a 0% tax rate, then there would be no tax revenue generated. Conversely, if a government imposes a 100% tax rate, then there would also be no tax revenue generated, as people would have no incentive to work or engage in economic activity. Therefore, there must be an optimal tax rate that maximizes tax revenue, somewhere between 0% and 100%.

As tax rates increase, people are less inclined to work, invest, and engage in economic activity, as they keep less of the income they generate. Therefore, tax revenue will decrease beyond a certain point. Conversely, if tax rates are too low, then there is less revenue generated, as there is less money being collected from each person.

The Laffer Curve concept is often used in discussions about tax policy and the optimal level of taxation. For example, if a government believes that tax rates are too low, it may decide to raise taxes to increase revenue. However, if the tax rate is already beyond the optimal point, then the tax increase may actually lead to a decrease in tax revenue.

An example of the Laffer Curve in action can be seen in the United States during the 1980s. President Reagan implemented a tax cut policy, which reduced tax rates across the board. Despite the lower tax rates, tax revenue actually increased, as the policy led to higher economic growth and increased economic activity. This is an example of how the Laffer Curve can be used to guide tax policy decisions.

Another example of the Laffer Curve can be seen in some countries that have implemented high tax rates, which have led to tax evasion, underground economies, and lower levels of economic activity. These countries may be beyond the optimal point on the Laffer Curve, which means that reducing tax rates could actually increase tax revenue.

Overall, the Laffer Curve concept is a useful tool for understanding the relationship between tax rates and tax revenue. However, it is important to consider other factors, such as government spending, economic growth, and income distribution, when making tax policy decisions. The optimal tax rate is not fixed, and it can vary depending on the specific circumstances of each country or region.

The Gini Coefficient - The Gini coefficient is a measure of income inequality within a population. It is calculated as a ratio between the area that lies between the Lorenz curve (a graphical representation of income distribution) and the diagonal line of perfect equality, to the total area under the diagonal line. The Gini coefficient ranges from 0 to 1, with 0 representing perfect equality and 1 representing perfect inequality.

For example, let's consider two different countries, Country A and Country B, and their respective Gini coefficients. Country A has a Gini coefficient of 0.25, while Country B has a Gini coefficient of 0.65. This indicates that Country B has a higher level of income inequality than Country A.

Another example could be the comparison of two different regions within a country. Let's consider the Gini coefficients of two states within India, Kerala and Uttar Pradesh. According to the latest data, Kerala has a Gini coefficient of 0.38, while Uttar Pradesh has a Gini coefficient of 0.40. This suggests that there is slightly higher income inequality in Uttar Pradesh than in Kerala.

The Gini coefficient is also used to analyse income inequality over time. For example, let's consider the Gini coefficients of the United States over the past few decades. In the 1960s, the Gini coefficient was around 0.38, indicating relatively low-income inequality. However, over the next few decades, income inequality increased, with the Gini coefficient reaching a peak of 0.49 in the late 2000s. In recent years, the Gini coefficient has decreased slightly, but it remains relatively high compared to historical levels.

The Gini coefficient can also be used to compare income inequality between different demographic groups. For example, in the United States, the Gini coefficient for women is slightly lower than the Gini coefficient for men, suggesting that there is slightly less income inequality among women. Additionally, the Gini coefficient for African Americans and Hispanic Americans is higher than for White Americans, indicating higher levels of income inequality for these groups.

Overall, the Gini coefficient is a useful tool for understanding income inequality within a population. However, it is important to consider other factors, such as poverty rates, social mobility, and access to education and healthcare, when analysing income inequality. Additionally, the Gini coefficient should be used in conjunction with other measures of inequality, such as the Palma ratio or the 90/10 ratio, to gain a more comprehensive understanding of income distribution.

The Prisoner's Dilemma - The Prisoner's Dilemma is a classic concept in game theory that demonstrates why two rational individuals might not cooperate, even when it is in their best interest to do so. The dilemma arises when two individuals must choose whether to cooperate with each other or act in their own self-interest. The outcome of the game depends on the choices made by both individuals.

Here is an example of the Prisoner's Dilemma:

Two criminals, A and B, are arrested and brought to separate rooms for interrogation. The prosecutor offers each of them a plea deal: if they confess and implicate the other person, they will receive a reduced sentence, but if both confess, they will both receive a longer sentence. If neither confesses, they will both receive a shorter sentence.

The dilemma arises because each criminal has to decide whether to cooperate with the other by remaining silent, or act in their own self-interest by confessing. If both remain silent, they will both receive a shorter sentence. However, if one confesses and implicates the other, they will receive an even shorter sentence, while the other will receive a longer one. If both confess, they will both receive a longer sentence.

Another example of the Prisoner's Dilemma can be found in international relations. Two countries, A and B, are considering whether to build up their military capabilities. If both countries invest in their military, it will lead to an arms race and a more dangerous world. If neither invests in their military, the world will be a safer place, but each country risks being vulnerable to attack. If one country invests in their military while the other does not, the country that invests will be better prepared for defence, but will have spent resources that could have been used elsewhere.

In both examples, the dilemma arises because the outcome depends on the choices made by both individuals (or countries). Each individual has an incentive to act in their own self-interest, but if both individuals do so, they will both end up worse off than if they had cooperated.

There are several possible strategies for resolving the Prisoner's Dilemma. One approach is to use punishment to deter defection. In the criminal example, the prosecutor could offer a reduced sentence to the person who cooperates with the other, but only if the other person remains silent. This would encourage both individuals to cooperate. In the international relations example, countries could agree to disarmament treaties to reduce the likelihood of an arms race.

Another approach is to establish trust between the two individuals (or countries) through repeated interactions. If two individuals know that they will interact with each other in the future, they may be more likely to cooperate, as defection in one round could lead to a loss of future benefits.

Overall, the Prisoner's Dilemma illustrates the challenges of cooperation in situations where individuals have conflicting incentives. It highlights the importance of trust and cooperation in achieving mutually beneficial outcomes.

The Invisible Hand - The Invisible Hand is a concept in economics introduced by Adam Smith in his book "The Wealth of Nations". The concept refers to the idea that individuals, by pursuing their own self-interest, can unintentionally benefit society as a whole. In other words, a free-market economy guided by the pursuit of self-interest of individuals and firms will result in an efficient allocation of resources and optimal economic outcomes.

The Invisible Hand concept works in the following way: when individuals pursue their own self-interest, they compete with each other in the marketplace for goods and services. Competition among buyers and sellers in the marketplace leads to price discovery, which helps to allocate resources efficiently. When goods and services are in high demand, the price goes up, which signals to producers to increase supply. Conversely, when demand is low, the price goes down, which signals to producers to decrease supply. As a result, market prices serve as signals for both producers and consumers, guiding them towards efficient allocation of resources.

One example of the Invisible Hand concept in action is the pricing mechanism in a free market economy. In a free market economy, prices are determined by supply and demand. When demand for a product increases, its price will rise. This signals to producers to increase production of that product. Conversely, if demand for a product decreases, its price will fall. This signals to producers to reduce production. As a result, the market is able to efficiently allocate resources based on the changing demands of consumers.

Another example of the Invisible Hand concept is the self-regulating nature of the market. In a free market economy, firms and individuals compete with each other. If a firm produces a product that is in high demand, other firms will enter the market to produce similar products, which leads to competition and innovation. Conversely, if a firm produces a product that is no longer in demand, it will either innovate to produce a new product or exit the market. As a result, the market is able to self-regulate and allocate resources efficiently.

However, it is important to note that the Invisible Hand concept assumes a perfectly competitive market with no externalities, such as pollution or social inequality. In reality, markets may be imperfect and may require government intervention to correct market failures and achieve optimal economic outcomes.

In conclusion, the Invisible Hand concept is a powerful idea that explains how a free-market economy can efficiently allocate resources based on the self-interest of individuals and firms. Its applications are vast and can be seen in many economic activities. However, its assumptions of a perfectly competitive market may not always hold true in reality, and government intervention may be necessary to achieve optimal outcomes.

Some interesting scientific concepts

Here are some interesting scientific concepts:

Schrodinger's Cat: Schrodinger's Cat is a thought experiment in quantum mechanics proposed by Austrian physicist Erwin Schrödinger in 1935. The experiment is intended to illustrate the strange and seemingly paradoxical nature of quantum mechanics, which describes the behaviour of subatomic particles.

The experiment involves a cat in a sealed box with a vial of poison and a radioactive source. The radioactive source has a 50% chance of decaying within a certain period of time, which triggers a mechanism that releases the poison and kills the cat. According to quantum mechanics, the radioactive decay is described by a probability distribution, meaning that until the box is opened and the outcome is observed, the decay is in a superposition of states, both decayed and not decayed, at the same time. Therefore, until the box is opened, the cat is both alive and dead at the same time, in a state called a "superposition".

The paradox arises when the box is opened and the state of the cat is observed. According to quantum mechanics, the act of observation "collapses" the wave function and the cat is either alive or dead, with no possibility of being in a superposition of states. The act of observation seems to have a real effect on the state of the system, which contradicts classical physics, where the act of measurement is seen as a passive process that does not affect the system being measured.

The Schrodinger's Cat thought experiment is often used to illustrate the concept of quantum entanglement, where particles can be correlated in such a way that the state of one particle affects the state of the other, even if they are separated by large distances. It is also used to highlight the limits of classical physics in explaining the behaviour of subatomic particles.

While the experiment is purely theoretical and has never been carried out in reality, it has become a popular metaphor for discussing the strange and counterintuitive nature of quantum mechanics.

Chaos Theory: Chaos Theory is a branch of mathematics that deals with the study of complex and dynamic systems that exhibit unpredictable and chaotic behaviour over time. The theory originated in the late 20th century as a response to the limitations of traditional linear models and has since found applications in a wide range of fields, including physics, biology, economics, and engineering.

At the heart of Chaos Theory is the idea that seemingly random and unpredictable behaviour can actually arise from underlying patterns and structures in complex systems. These patterns can give rise to what is known as the "butterfly effect", where small changes in the initial conditions of a system can led to large and unpredictable outcomes over time.

One of the key concepts in Chaos Theory is the idea of "strange attractors", which are patterns or structures in a chaotic system that govern the long-term behaviour of the system. These attractors can be thought of as regions in the system's state space that the system tends to move towards over time, even though the behaviour within these regions may be highly unpredictable and chaotic.

Another important concept in Chaos Theory is that of "fractals", which are complex, self-similar patterns that repeat at different scales. Fractals are often found in chaotic systems, and they can provide insights into the underlying patterns and structures that govern the system's behaviour.

Chaos Theory has many practical applications, including weather forecasting, the study of ecological systems, financial modelling, and the design of control systems for complex machinery. By understanding the underlying patterns and structures that govern chaotic systems, scientists and engineers can better predict and control their behaviour, leading to more efficient and effective systems.

One of the most famous examples of Chaos Theory in action is the weather. Weather patterns are highly complex and dynamic, with many interacting factors such as temperature, humidity, air pressure, and wind. The behaviour of these factors over time is highly unpredictable and can lead to chaotic weather patterns such as hurricanes and tornadoes. However, by using Chaos Theory to model these patterns and identify the underlying structures and patterns, meteorologists can make more accurate predictions about future weather events.

Chaos Theory is a powerful and highly interdisciplinary field of study that has revolutionized our understanding of complex and dynamic systems. Its concepts and techniques have found applications in a wide range of fields and have led to important advances in our ability to predict and control the behaviour of these systems.

Black Hole: Black holes are one of the most fascinating and enigmatic objects in the universe. They are formed from the remnants of massive stars that have collapsed under the weight of their own gravity, creating a singularity at their core, which is an infinitely dense and small point.

According to the theory of general relativity, a black hole is a region of space-time where gravity is so strong that nothing, not even light, can escape its pull. The boundary around the black hole from which nothing can escape is known as the event horizon. Once an object crosses the event horizon, it is irreversibly pulled into the black hole and is lost forever.

The concept of black holes was first introduced in the 18th century by John Michell and Pierre-Simon Laplace, but it was not until the 20th century that their existence was confirmed through observations and experiments. Today, black holes are one of the most active areas of research in astrophysics, as they are believed to play a crucial role in the evolution of galaxies and the universe itself.

Black holes come in different sizes, ranging from micro black holes with masses less than the moon to supermassive black holes with masses millions or billions of times that of the sun. The size of a black hole is determined by its mass, with larger black holes having a stronger gravitational pull and a larger event horizon.

One of the most intriguing aspects of black holes is the phenomenon of Hawking radiation. According to this theory proposed by physicist Stephen Hawking in 1974, black holes emit radiation due to quantum effects near the event horizon, causing them to slowly evaporate over time. This process is incredibly slow for large black holes, taking trillions of years to evaporate, but for smaller black holes, it can occur much faster.

In addition to their scientific importance, black holes have captured the popular imagination and have been featured in countless works of science fiction and popular culture. They continue to be a subject of intense study and fascination for scientists and the public alike.

Entropy: Entropy is a fundamental concept in thermodynamics and statistical mechanics that refers to the amount of disorder or randomness in a system. It is a measure of the number of ways that the particles in a system can be arranged, and it increases as the system becomes more disordered.

The concept of entropy was first introduced by the German physicist Rudolf Clausius in the 19th century to explain the behavior of heat engines. He observed that in any heat transfer process, there is always some energy that is lost or wasted, and that this energy is related to the disorder or entropy of the system.

Entropy is represented by the symbol S and is measured in units of joules per kelvin. It is related to the number of possible microstates or arrangements of particles in a system, and is given by the equation $S = k \ln W$, where k is the Boltzmann constant and W is the number of possible microstates.

One of the key features of entropy is that it always increases in isolated systems, according to the second law of thermodynamics. This means that over time, the amount of energy available to do useful work in a closed system will decrease as the system becomes more disordered.

Entropy has many important applications in physics, chemistry, and engineering. It is used to analyse the efficiency of energy conversion processes, such as power plants and engines, and to understand the behaviour of complex systems such as fluids, materials, and biological systems.

Entropy also has important implications for information theory, where it is used to quantify the amount of uncertainty or randomness in a message or signal. This has applications in areas such as data compression, cryptography, and communication systems.

Entropy is a fundamental concept in science that describes the amount of disorder or randomness in a system. It is related to the number of possible arrangements of particles in a system and always increases in isolated systems, reflecting the second law of thermodynamics. Entropy has numerous applications in physics, chemistry, engineering, and information theory, making it a critical concept for understanding the behaviour of complex systems.

Heisenberg's Uncertainty Principle: Heisenberg's Uncertainty Principle, also known as the Principle of Indeterminacy, is a fundamental concept in quantum mechanics that states that it is impossible to simultaneously determine certain pairs of physical properties of a subatomic particle, such as its position and momentum, with absolute precision.

In more technical terms, the principle can be mathematically expressed as:

$$\Delta x * \Delta p >= h/4\pi$$

where Δx is the uncertainty in position, Δp is the uncertainty in momentum, h is Planck's constant, and π is pi.

This principle has important implications for the behaviour of particles at the quantum level. It implies that, for example, the more precisely we try to measure the position of a particle, the less precisely we can know its momentum, and vice versa. In other words, the more accurately we know one property, the less accurately we can know the other.

The Uncertainty Principle is often illustrated by the famous thought experiment of a photon or an electron passing through a pair of slits. When we observe the particle's path through the slits, we can determine its position with great accuracy, but we will lose information about its momentum. Conversely, if we try to measure its momentum, we will lose information about its position.

The Uncertainty Principle has been verified by numerous experiments, and is considered a fundamental aspect of the behavior of subatomic particles. It is also important in fields such as quantum computing and cryptography, where the limits of measurement and observation are important considerations.

Doppler Effect: The Doppler Effect is a phenomenon observed in waves, such as light and sound waves, where the frequency and wavelength of the wave are affected by the motion of the source or observer.

In the case of sound waves, the Doppler Effect can be observed when a moving object, such as a car or an airplane, emits a sound wave. As the object moves toward an observer, the sound waves are compressed, resulting in a higher frequency and a shorter wavelength. This causes the sound to appear higher-pitched than it actually is. Conversely, as the object moves away from an observer, the sound waves are stretched, resulting in a lower frequency and a longer wavelength. This causes the sound to appear lower-pitched than it actually is.

For example, imagine standing by the side of a road while a car approaches you with its horn blaring. As the car gets closer, the pitch of the horn seems to increase, becoming higher and shriller. Once the car passes you and begins moving away, the pitch of the horn seems to decrease, becoming lower and more muffled.

The Doppler Effect can also be observed in light waves. For example, as a star moves closer to or further away from Earth, the light it emits can appear shifted toward the blue or red end of the spectrum, respectively. This is known as the blueshift or redshift, and is caused by the Doppler Effect on the light waves.

The Doppler Effect has many practical applications, including in the measurement of blood flow and in radar technology. In medicine, the Doppler Effect is used to measure the speed and direction of blood flow through the body, which can help diagnose conditions such as blood clots and blockages. In radar technology, the Doppler Effect is used to measure the speed and direction of objects, such as airplanes and weather systems, and is an important tool for weather forecasting and air traffic control.

Higgs Boson: The Higgs boson is a subatomic particle in particle physics. It is a fundamental particle and is named after Peter Higgs, a physicist who first theorized its existence in 1964. The Higgs boson is a vital component in the Standard Model of particle physics, which explains the fundamental particles that make up the universe and the forces that govern their interactions.

The Higgs boson is responsible for giving particles mass. According to the Standard Model, particles gain mass by interacting with a Higgs field that permeates all of space. Particles that interact more strongly with the Higgs field have a higher mass, while those that interact less strongly have a lower mass. The Higgs boson is the particle associated with this field.

The existence of the Higgs boson was finally confirmed in 2012 by experiments at the Large Hadron Collider (LHC) in Switzerland. Scientists used the LHC to smash protons together at very high energies, creating a shower of particles. By analysing the properties of these particles, researchers were able to identify the signature of the Higgs boson.

The discovery of the Higgs boson was a major breakthrough in particle physics, and it confirmed one of the central predictions of the Standard Model. It also opened up new avenues for research into the nature of the universe and the fundamental forces that govern it.

The Higgs boson has important implications for our understanding of the early universe. In the moments after the Big Bang, the universe was a hot, dense soup of particles. As the universe cooled, the Higgs field kicked in, giving particles mass and allowing them to clump together to form atoms, stars, and galaxies. Without the Higgs boson, the universe as we know it today would not exist.

The Higgs boson is a fundamental particle that gives other particles mass. Its discovery was a major breakthrough in particle physics, confirming a central prediction of the Standard Model and opening up new avenues for research into the nature of the universe.

Dark Matter: Dark matter is a hypothetical form of matter that is believed to exist in the universe. It is called "dark" because it does not interact with light or any other form of electromagnetic radiation, making it invisible to telescopes and other instruments that detect electromagnetic radiation. Its presence can only be inferred from its gravitational effects on visible matter.

The concept of dark matter arose from observations of galaxies and clusters of galaxies. When astronomers observed the motion of stars and gas within a galaxy or cluster, they found that the observed gravitational force was not strong enough to hold the objects together. There simply wasn't enough visible matter in the galaxy or cluster to account for the observed motion. It was as if there was some invisible matter that was providing the additional gravitational force needed to keep everything in place.

The existence of dark matter was first proposed in the 1930s by Swiss astronomer Fritz Zwicky, who noticed discrepancies in the observed mass of galaxy clusters. However, it wasn't until the 1970s that the concept gained widespread acceptance among astronomers.

There are several different types of evidence for the existence of dark matter. One type of evidence comes from the observation of gravitational lensing, which occurs when the gravitational field of a massive object, such as a galaxy cluster, bends the light from more distant objects. The amount of bending can be used to determine the mass of the gravitational lens, and in some cases, the amount of mass inferred from the lensing is much greater than the amount of visible matter in the cluster, suggesting the presence of dark matter.

Another type of evidence comes from the observation of the cosmic microwave background radiation, which is thought to be the leftover radiation from the Big Bang. The pattern of temperature fluctuations in the cosmic microwave background can be used to infer the distribution of matter in the early universe. The observed pattern is consistent with the presence of dark matter, which would have influenced the distribution of matter in the early universe through its gravitational effects.

Despite its importance in the structure and evolution of the universe, the nature of dark matter remains a mystery. There are several candidates for what dark matter might be, including exotic particles such as WIMPs (weakly interacting massive particles) and axions. However, none of these candidates have been definitively identified, and the search for dark matter continues to be a major focus of research in astrophysics and particle physics.

Cryptography

Cryptography is the practice of secure communication in the presence of third parties. It involves the use of codes and ciphers to protect information, ensuring that only authorized parties can access it. Cryptography has been used for centuries to keep sensitive information confidential and secure, such as military or diplomatic communications.

There are two main types of cryptography: symmetric-key cryptography and public-key cryptography. In symmetric-key cryptography, the same key is used for encryption and decryption of a message, whereas in public-key cryptography, a public key is used for encryption and a private key is used for decryption.

Here are some examples of cryptography:

Caesar Cipher: A simple substitution cipher in which each letter in the plaintext is replaced by a letter a fixed number of positions down the alphabet. For example, with a shift of 3, A would be replaced by D, B would become E, and so on.

Enigma Machine: A complex electro-mechanical device used by the Germans during World War II to encrypt and decrypt messages. The machine used a series of rotating rotors to substitute letters, making it extremely difficult to crack.

RSA: A widely used public-key cryptography algorithm developed by Ron Rivest, Adi Shamir, and Leonard Adleman in the late 1970s. RSA is based on the mathematical difficulty of factoring large numbers, and uses a public key for encryption and a private key for decryption.

AES: A symmetric-key encryption algorithm that is widely used for encrypting sensitive data, such as financial transactions or personal information. AES is a block cipher, meaning it encrypts data in fixed-size blocks.

SSL/TLS: Secure Socket Layer (SSL) and its successor Transport Layer Security (TLS) are cryptographic protocols used to provide secure communication over the internet. SSL/TLS encrypts data between a web server and a client, preventing eavesdropping and tampering. It is widely used for online transactions, such as online banking and e-commerce.

Cryptography is an important tool for protecting sensitive information in today's digital world. Its applications are broad, ranging from secure communication to digital signatures and authentication.

While cryptography is a powerful tool for protecting sensitive information, there are also some risks associated with its use. Here are some of the main risks of cryptography:

Key management: Cryptography relies on the secure storage and management of encryption keys. If encryption keys are compromised, attackers can potentially decrypt sensitive information. Organizations must ensure that encryption keys are securely stored and managed to prevent unauthorized access.

Algorithm weaknesses: Cryptographic algorithms can be vulnerable to attack if weaknesses are discovered in their design or implementation. If a cryptographic algorithm is found to be weak, attackers can exploit this vulnerability to decrypt messages or otherwise compromise the system.

Malware: Malicious software, such as keyloggers or spyware, can be used to steal encryption keys or other sensitive information. Organizations must ensure that their systems are protected against malware and that users are trained to recognize and avoid common malware threats.

Quantum computing: While current cryptographic algorithms are considered secure against classical computing attacks, the development of quantum computers could potentially break many current encryption schemes. Cryptographers are actively researching and developing new cryptographic algorithms that are resistant to quantum computing attacks.

Human error: Cryptography is a complex field that requires expertise to use correctly. Human errors, such as misconfiguration or mismanagement of encryption keys, can result in the compromise of sensitive information. Organizations must ensure that their staff are trained in the proper use and management of cryptographic systems.

Algorithmic trading

Algorithmic trading, also known as algo trading or black-box trading, is a method of executing financial transactions using automated computer algorithms. Algorithmic trading can be used for a variety of financial instruments, including stocks, options, futures, and currencies.

The basic idea behind algorithmic trading is to use a set of predefined rules and mathematical models to analyse market data and make trading decisions. These algorithms can be designed to execute trades automatically based on specific market conditions or other factors.

Here are some detailed examples of algorithmic trading:

Trend-following strategies: These algorithms analyse historical price data and attempt to identify trends in the market. For example, a trend-following algorithm might buy a stock when its price rises above its moving average, and sell it when its price falls below its moving average.

Mean-reversion strategies: These algorithms look for deviations from the average price of a financial instrument and attempt to capitalize on those deviations. For example, a mean-reversion algorithm might buy a stock when its price falls below its historical average, and sell it when its price rises above its historical average.

Statistical arbitrage: These algorithms look for mispricing between related financial instruments and attempt to profit from those mispricing. For example, a statistical arbitrage algorithm might buy one stock and short sell another stock that it believes is overvalued relative to the first stock.

High-frequency trading: These algorithms attempt to profit from small price movements in the market by executing trades at a very high frequency. High-frequency trading algorithms can execute trades in fractions of a second, and rely on speed and low latency to gain an advantage over other market participants.

Overall, algorithmic trading has become increasingly popular in financial markets due to its ability to execute trades quickly and efficiently, and its potential to generate profits using sophisticated mathematical models and data analysis techniques.

While algorithmic trading can provide a number of benefits, such as increased efficiency and faster execution of trades, there are also some negative sides to algorithmic trading. Here are a few of the potential drawbacks of algorithmic trading:

Increased market volatility: Algorithmic trading can increase market volatility by amplifying market movements. For example, if an algorithm detects a downward trend in a stock's price, it may automatically trigger a sell order, which can lead to a sharp drop in the stock's price. This can create a feedback loop where other algorithms detect the price drop and trigger additional sell orders, leading to further price declines.

Systematic risk: Algorithmic trading can create systematic risk if a large number of algorithms are programmed to execute similar trades based on the same market data. This can lead to a situation where a single market event can trigger a cascade of automated trades, leading to a market crash or other significant market disruption.

Algorithmic errors: Algorithms can contain errors or bugs that can lead to unexpected or unintended trading behavior. For example, a faulty algorithm might execute trades based on incorrect market data or fail to execute trades in a timely manner, resulting in losses for the trader.

Lack of transparency: Algorithmic trading can be opaque, with trades executed automatically by computer algorithms without human intervention. This can make it difficult to understand the trading decisions being made and to ensure that algorithms are behaving in a responsible manner.

Ethical concerns: Algorithmic trading can raise ethical concerns, particularly when it comes to high-frequency trading. Critics argue that high-frequency traders are able to use their speed advantage to exploit inefficiencies in the market, to the detriment of other market participants.

While algorithmic trading can provide significant benefits to traders, investors, and the market as a whole, it also comes with potential risks and drawbacks that should be carefully considered. It is important to manage these risks through careful design and monitoring of algorithms, and to ensure that algorithmic trading is used in a responsible and transparent manner.

9 798890 023537

Printed by Libri Plureos GmbH in Hamburg, Germany